EDITOR: MARTIN WINDROW

OSPREY MILITARY

ELITE SERIES

41

ELITE FORCES OF INDIA AND PAKISTAN

KEN CONBOY

Colour plates by

PAUL HANNON

Published in 1992 by
Osprey Publishing Ltd
59 Grosvenor Street, London W1X 9DA
© Copyright 1992 Osprey Publishing Ltd

ISBN 185532 209 9

Filmset in Great Britain
Printed through Bookbuilders Ltd, Hong Kong

Editor's Note

This volume also details the Elite Forces of
Afghanistan, Bangladesh, Nepal and Sri
Lanka.

Readers may like to note that in 1991 the
Indian Marine Special Forces (IMSF) were
renamed the Marine Commando Force.

Acknowledgements

The author would like to thank the following for their
assistance: Shekhar Gupta, Vivek Nehru, K. K.
Nayyar, Embassy of Pakistan (Washington), Embassy
of India (Washington), and many others who would
rather remain anonymous.

INDIA: ARMY AIRBORNE

Influenced by the German use of paratroopers early in World War Two, Gen. Sir Robert Cassels, the Commander-in-Chief India, ordered the formation of an airborne cadre in October 1940. The cadre was to consist of British, Indian, and Gorkha[1] troops, and would be used as the basis for a mixed airborne brigade. Two months later Cassels further ordered the formation of three parachute battalions. However, because of equipment and aircraft shortages, London would not consent to the formation of Indian paratroop units. It was not until June 1941 that the British War Office approved plans for three airborne battalions to be raised in India, provided that one was British.

With London's consent, 50 Indian Parachute Brigade was officially formed in October 1941. It was located in Delhi, while a new Airlanding School was opened nearby at Willingdon Airport, New Delhi. The initial units in the brigade were 151 British, 152 Indian and 153 Gorkha Parachute Battalions. All were volunteers, and most of the brigade's officers were British.

The brigade's first experimental jump was conducted at Karachi on 15 October 1941. The first brigade exercise took place in February 1942. Few parachutes were available, but the troops were put through extensive ground training. Three small

(1) 'Gorkha' is the spelling used in India; in Nepal and Britain it is spelled 'Gurkha'. During World War Two, there were ten regiments of Gorkhas in the British Indian Army; currently, there are seven regiments of Gorkhas in the Indian Army.

A stick of paratroopers from 152 Para Battalion line up outside a C-47 Dakota, circa 1943. Note the British-style wings on the shoulder, and knit headgear.

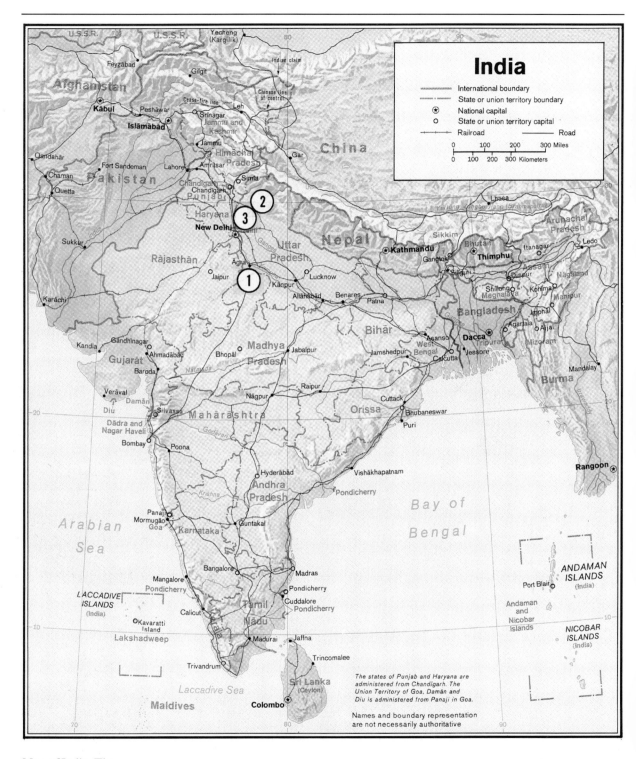

Map of India. The Parachute Regiment is located at Agra (1). The Special Frontier Force has its training camp at Chakrata (2) and airbase at Sarasawa (3).

airborne operations were undertaken during this time. In July 1942 a company from 152 Indian Para Bn. was dropped in the Sind in an unsuccessful attempt to neutralize rebellious tribesmen. During the same month 11 officers and men from the brigade were dropped at Myitkyina, Burma, to gather intelligence on Japanese forces. In August, 11 more officers and men were dropped in Burma to repair the airfield facilities at Fort Herz.

In October 1942 151 British Para Bn. departed the brigade and was sent to the Middle East. During the same month the Airlanding School was renamed the Parachute Training School and moved to Chaklala, and 50 Indian Para Bde. was moved to Campbellpur, about 50 miles west of Chaklala. In early 1943 the brigade was given another Gorkha battalion to bring it up to strength. In addition, C-47 Dakotas began supporting the Parachute Training School. In September 1943 the decision was made to form a mixed Indian airborne division as soon as a British parachute brigade could be sent from the Middle East or Europe. Because a British brigade could not be spared the new Indian formation, called 9 Indian Airborne Division, was given only a skeleton staff.

In March 1944 50 Indian Para Bde. was placed under 23 Indian Infantry Division and used successfully to repel a Japanese ground attack in north-eastern India. Fighting lasted until July, and the brigade was singled out for special mention for its actions at Imphal and Kohima.

During March, while 50 Para Bde. was being rushed to the north-east, the skeleton 9 Indian Abn. Div. was renamed 44 Indian Abn. Div. and given a fresh infusion of officers. The new division was given 14 Brigade (because of its previous experience in the Chindit operations, this British formation was renamed 14 Airlanding Brigade). 50 Indian Para Bde., the division's second brigade, was posted to Rawalpindi. In January 1945 the division received 77 Para Bde., which was also a veteran British Chindit unit.

In December 1944 the British government authorized the formation of the Indian Parachute Regiment. In the Indian system, like its British model, regiments act as a headquarters for training and recruitment. In this way the parachute regiment could raise and train its own Indian and Gorkha battalions for the Airborne Division's two parachute brigades. The regiment was initially tasked with providing four parachute battalions[2]; the remaining battalions in the division were British.

On 30 April 1945, with many of its officers and men on leave, a

(2) These were built around the one Indian and two Gorkha parachute battalions that already existed in 50 Indian Para Bde.

Order of Battle, 44 Indian Airborne Division, July 1945

50 Indian Para Brigade
16 Para Bn. (British)
1 Indian Para Bn.
3 Gorkha Para Bn.

77 Indian Para Brigade
15 Para Bn. (British)
2 Gorkha Para Bn.
4 Indian Para Bn.
44 (British) Independent Pathfinder Coy.

14 Airlanding Brigade
2 Black Watch (British)
4 Rajputana Rifles
6/16 Punjab Regt.

Recce
44 Indian Airborne Div. Recce Sqn.

Support
Four engineer squadrons, a signals unit, two light artillery/AAA units, one supply company, three transport companies, four medical units, and a division workshop.

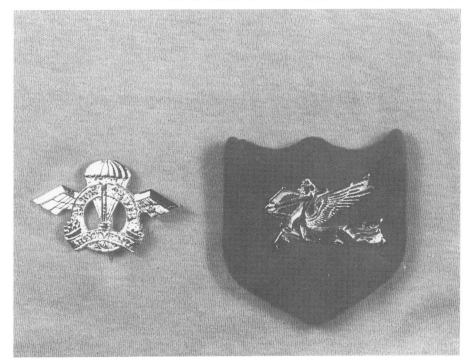

Indian Parachute insignia. In 1952, the Parachute Regt. created a new white metal cap badge (left). During World War Two the cap badge of the old Indian Parachute Regt. resembled that of the British Parachute Regt., with the addition of an Ashok lion at the top and the word 'India' at the bottom. Also in 1952, 50 Independent Para Bde. adopted a new formation insignia featuring the winged Shatrujeet from Hindu mythology (right), in white metal on maroon. Prior to 1952, the formation sign for 50 Independent Para Bde., conceived by the British, featured Pegasus.

composite parachute battalion from the division was put together and parachuted at Tawhai during operations to recapture Burma from Japanese forces.

With the end of World War Two, 44 Indian Abn. Div. moved in October 1945 to new quarters at Karachi. Along with the change in location, the division was renamed 2 Indian Airborne Division.

Partition

Following the war, plans were forwarded for the demobilization of significant portions of the Indian Army. While it was recommended that the airborne division be retained, the parachute regiment was to be disbanded. In addition, the British were committed to gradually nationalizing the Indian Army. As a result, British troops were removed from the parachute brigades, as were some British officers. Gorkha troops, too, were removed from the division. Finally, 14 Airlanding Bde. was converted into 14 Parachute Brigade. On 26 October 1946 the Indian Parachute Regiment was officially disbanded. Without its own training and recruitment headquarters, the Airborne Division had to rely on selected infantry regiments to supply battalions. Once received, these battalions would then be put through airborne training by the division. The new organization of 2 Indian Abn. Div. was as follows:

Division Headquarters
1 Bn., Kumaon Regiment
3 Bn., 15 Punjab Regiment
14 Parachute Brigade
1 Bn., Frontier Force Regiment
3 Bn., 16 Punjab Regiment
4 Bn., 6 Rajputana Rifles Regiment
50 Parachute Brigade
3 Bn., 1 Punjab Regiment

3 Bn., Baluch Regiment
2 Bn., Madras Regiment
77 Parachute Brigade
1 Bn., 2 Punjab Regiment
3 Bn., Maratha Light Infantry Regiment
3 Bn., Rajput Regiment

In February 1947 the British announced their intention of leaving India by June 1948. Unprecedented communal violence between Hindu and Muslim communities forced the airborne division to be used in internal security operations.

On 14 August 1947 India became a sovereign state; at the same time a divided Pakistan was born as an independent Muslim nation. In the partitioned subcontinent, India was granted two-thirds of the old Indian Army while Pakistan received one-third. The airborne division was divided between them: its headquarters, 50 and 77 Para Bdes. went to India, while 14 Para Bde. went to Pakistan. However, the parachute battalions did not necessarily follow the division headquarters or brigades, but rather took the lead of their parent regiments, which in turn were divided between the two states. Thus, within the division headquarters, 1 Bn., Kumaon Regt. remained with India, while 3 Bn., 15 Punjab Regt. went to Pakistan. All three battalions of 77 Para Bde. went to India, while in 14 Para Bde. all but 4 Bn., Rajputana Rifles went to Pakistan. In 50 Para Bde. only 3 Bn., Madras Regt. stayed with India.

Within a month of partition a crisis developed in relations between India and Pakistan over future control of the border state of Jammu and Kashmir. Open conflict broke out on 22 October 1947; five days later the headquarters of 2 Abn. Div., which had moved to Dehra Dun after partition, sent its 1 Bn., Kumaon Regt. to Srinagar to confront the Pakistanis. The two parachute brigades, meanwhile, were engaged in refugee evacuations elsewhere in the country. By November both brigades had been shifted to Jammu and Kashmir. Sporadic fighting lasted until the

Mountain division insignia: 2 Mountain Division (left), yellow on black; 3 Mountain Division (right), yellow, red and white on black.

Battle and Theatre Honours, 1947–1965

1 Para Bn.:	Theatre Honours (Jammu and Kashmir, 1947–48)
	Theatre Honours (Jammu and Kashmir, 1965)
	Battle Honours (Punch, 1947–48)
	Battle Honours (Hajipur, 1965)
2 Para Bn.:	Theatre Honours (Jammu and Kashmir, 1947–48)
	Battle Honours (Srinagar, Naushera, and Jhanger, 1947–48)
3 Para Bn.:	Theatre Honours (Jammu and Kashmir, 1947–48)
	Battle Honours (Punch, 1947–48)
411 Para Field Coy:	Theatre Honours (Jammu and Kashmir, 1947–48)

end of 1948, with the paratroopers used in a normal infantry role. A United Nations ceasefire ended hostilities in Kashmir on 1 January 1949.

After the ceasefire the paratroopers underwent major reorganization. 50 Para Bde. was moved to Ranchi in Bihar State, and placed under 5 Inf. Div. until August 1949, after which it was made independent and placed under the Eastern Command. In November 1949 a new Parachute Training School was opened at Agra[3]. In November 1950 India decided to retain only one parachute brigade, and 77 Para Bde. reverted to an infantry role. In addition, three of India's six parachute battalions reverted to infantry battalions[4]. The three remaining parachute battalions, placed under 50 Independent Para Bde., were permanently separated from their parent regiments to reform a Parachute Regiment at Agra. The new regiment was officially created on 15 April 1952; on that day, the three battalions were redesignated, 1 Bn., Punjab Regt. becoming 1 Bn., Para Regt.; 3 Bn., Maratha LI becoming 2 Bn., and 1 Bn., Kumaon Regt. becoming 3 Battalion.

Korea and the Middle East

In March 1951 India sent 60 Para Field Ambulance, a medical support unit within 50 Independent Para Bde., to Korea to serve with the United Nations forces. During that month the unit jumped with the US 187 Regimental Combat Team at Munsan, 25 miles north-west of Seoul. Over the following week the Indian medics treated more than 400 men. In September 1953 2 Para Bn. was sent to Korea to help oversee prison camps after the armistice. The battalion left Korea in February 1954. Upon its return it was posted to Agra, which became the new home of 50 Independent Para Bde.

In November 1956, following the Arab-Israeli War, 3 Para Bn. was sent to the Middle East for peace-keeping duties. One year later it was replaced by 1 Para Bn.

In 1957, and again in 1961, the Parachute Regt. established recruitment quotas based on geographical and ethnic background for each battalion. Based on these quotas, 1 Para Bn. contained a mix of Dogras, Sikhs, and other peoples from the Indian plains; 2 Para Bn. had a mix of Marathas, southern Indians, and Bengalis; and 3 Para Bn. a mix of Kumaons and other hill peoples. The regiment expanded slightly in June 1960 when the President's Bodyguard was airborne-qualified and designated the Pathfinder Squadron of 50 Independent Para Bde.; in addition, 4 Para Bn., consisting of Gorkhas, Dogras, Garwhalis, and south Indians, was raised in August 1961.

Goa

In November 1961 the Indian Army formulated plans to take the Portuguese colony of Goa, located on the Indian coast about 250 miles south of Bombay. The operation, codenamed 'Vijay', called for elements of 17 Inf. Div. and paratroopers to overwhelm the estimated 4,500 defenders. The Portuguese, expecting an airborne assault, had dispersed their troops and armour. Instead, 1 and 2 Para Bns. moved into Goa on foot beginning on 17 December; by the next morning the paras were accepting the surrender of the Portuguese troops. Final capitulation came later that morning.

The China War

By early 1961 the border between India and China was growing tense. Elements of the para brigade patrolled the Chinese frontier for the remainder of the year. When war erupted in October 1962, none of the para battalions were sent to battle. The only airborne unit committed was 17 Para Field Regt., an artillery formation attached to 50 Independent Para Bde. On 6 October men from the regiment were flown by helicopter to the frontline in the north-east, where they brought two field guns into action. This section was eventually overrun and taken prisoner. The remainder of the regiment was employed in the defence of the border town of Walong.

India was soundly defeated in its month-long confrontation with the Chinese. A period of rapid military expansion ensued, resulting in the creation of 5 Para Bn. in January 1963 and 6 Para Bn. in February 1963. 5 Para Bn. was attached to 61 Mountain Brigade, and 6 Para Bn. was posted to the new 58 Infantry Brigade. In October 1964 the Parachute Regiment raised 7 Para Bn.; this unit was placed in 50 Independent Para Bde. until the September 1965 war with Pakistan; after that it was removed from the brigade and replaced by 6 Para Bn. In January 1965 8 Para Bn. was formed and, nine months later, sent off to fight against Pakistan.

The Mountain Divisions

When relations with China first began to deteriorate in 1959, India took steps to create entire formations of acclimatized troops to fight along the Tibetan frontier. By the end of the year 4 Inf. Div. was moved to Assam and given responsibility for the border from Bhutan to Burma. The division's 11 Bde. was sent to Sikkim, while 7 and 5 Bdes. were posted to Arunachal. All of these units came under the army's 33 Corps, which was formed to control units in the north-east.

In September 1962 the Indian Army created the new 4 Corps as a second command structure to oversee units in the north-east. Neither of these corps was able to avert India's embarrassing defeat by China in October and November.

Immediately following the war India began a massive expansion to raise entire new mountain divisions. Mountain divisions differed from normal infantry divisions in several ways. First,

---

(3) The old Parachute Training School had gone to Pakistan after partition.
(4) 2 Bn., Madras Regt.; 4 Bn., 6 Rajputana Rifles; and 3 Bn., Rajput Regiment.

because of transportation problems, mountain divisions had no attached armoured units. Second, transportation elements were limited to smaller trucks and pack animals. Third, artillery consisted mainly of smaller 75mm pack howitzers and mortars. Fourth, troops assigned to mountain divisions were acclimatized in order to be able to fight at high altitude. In order to arm the new mountain divisions quickly, India received major infusions of equipment from the US and Britain; and these divisions were given preference when the British 7.62 Self-Loading Rifle began arriving in 1963.

Battalions from all infantry regiments are rotated through the mountain divisions. Each division is composed of three mountain brigades. Elite detachments of ski troops are sent from the divisions to the Winter Warfare School at Gunmark, which was expanded and renamed the High Altitude Warfare School following the 1962 war.

By 1966, there were a total of twelve mountain divisions:

2 Mountain Division Raised in 1962 and located in the extreme north-east of Arunachal Pradesh state; headquarters is in Dibrugarh. It belongs to 4 Corps, headquartered in Agartala.

3 Mountain Division Created in October 1962 in Ladakh. Fought in the 1965 War. In 1991 the division was part of 15 Corps of the Northern Command.

4 Mountain Division India's first infantry division to see combat in World War Two. Converted to a mountain division in 1963.

Fought in the 1965 War. Currently a reserve mountain division, headquartered in the lowlands at Allahabad (Uttar Pradesh).

5 Mountain Division Converted to a mountain division in 1963. Posted to the west of 2 Mtn. Div. in Arunachal Pradesh.

6 Mountain Division A new division raised in 1963. Originally headquartered in Naini Tal, west of Nepal; headquarters now shifted to Bareilly.

8 Mountain Division Raised in 1963 for counter-insurgency operations in Nagaland. Until 1990, headquartered in Kohima under 3 Corps of Eastern Command.

17 Mountain Division Raised in 1959 and converted to a mountain division in 1963. Assigned to the Sikkim sector. Currently headquartered in Gangtok and assigned to 33 Corps (headquartered in Siliguri).

20 Mountain Division Raised in 1963 and assigned to the Sikkim sector.

21 Mountain Division Raised in 1963 and assigned to Aranachal Pradesh, west of 5 Mountain Division.

23 Mountain Division Raised in 1963; a reserve mountain division headquartered in the plains at Ranchi, Bihar state.

27 Mountain Division Converted to a mountain division in 1963. Headquartered in Kalimpong and assigned to the Sikkim sector.

57 Mountain Division Raised in 1966 for counter-insurgency operations in Mizoram. Until 1990, headquartered in Aizawi under 3 Corps of Eastern Command.

THE 1965 WAR

In 1965 Indo-Pakistani relations once again deteriorated. Tension was focused in the contested Rann of Kutch, a salt-covered desert along the southernmost portion of the Indo-Pakistani border. Skirmishes took place on 9 April; two days later 2 Para Bn. was sent to the front; 3 Para Bn. joined it on 18 April, and 4 Para Bn. on 24 April. After two months of limited fighting, hostilities ceased on 30 June; all the para battalions were withdrawn from the Rann of Kutch by the first week of August.

As fighting in the Rann of Kutch was winding down, tension began to increase in the disputed state of Kashmir. Beginning on 5 August, Pakistani-trained guerrillas, codenamed 'Gibraltar Forces', began infiltrating into Kashmir. While the guerrillas succeeded in creating some confusion, the anticipated uprising by the Muslim majority of Kashmiris did not occur.

During the second week of August the Indian Army was sent to seal the border of Kashmir. Among the forces already on hand in Kashmir was 1 Para Bn., which had been stationed there since November 1963. On 23 August the battalion was put under the control of 68 Inf. Bde. Two days later the paratroopers moved against the strategic Haji Pir Pass, one of the most important routes from Pakistan to Kashmir. Leading the drive through heavy rains during the early morning hours of 28 August, the battalion stormed down on the Pakistani defenders and took the pass by 1030 hours. The paratroopers then pushed the Pakistanis off a position 1,500 yards to the south-west of the pass on 30 August.

After the guerrilla operation into Kashmir failed Pakistan launched on 1 September 'Operation Grandslam', a combined armour-infantry attack into the Chhamb sector near Akhur in the state of Kashmir. By 6 September India was responding with cross-border thrusts toward Lahore. Alerted for deployment on 7 September, 50 Independent Para Bde. was placed upon arrival in Punjab under 15 Inf. Div. In heavy fighting over the next week, 2, 3, and 6 Para Bns. captured a series of bridges in the Lahore sector. A ceasefire was called on 23 September, after which the brigade was ordered to relieve an infantry brigade. On 1 November the brigade was withdrawn.

During the brief war 8 Para Bn., which was not assigned to 50 Independent Para Bde. at the time, moved from Agra to the Punjab, but saw no action. On 21 November the battalion was sent to Gwalior, where it joined 51 Independent Para Bde., which had been forming since 1 April 1965. 4 Para Bn., which was posted to 63 Mtn. Bde., operated in Sikkim to counter any possible Chinese incursions during the war with Pakistan. 5 Para Bn. remained in Nagaland attached to 61 Mtn. Bde.; 7 Para Bn. moved to Dharchula on the Uttar Pradesh-China border in late September, where it became part of 51 Independent Para Bde.

Several of India's mountain divisions saw action during the war. Elements of 3 Mtn. Div. were used in the Ladakh sector, their normal area of operations. In addition, one mountain division was assigned to each of the two army corps involved in the counter-offensives against Pakistan: in I Corps, 6 Mtn. Div. was shifted from its area of operations to the west of Nepal to the Sialkot sector; in II Corps, 4 Mtn. Div. was ordered to attack in the Lahore sector.

After the ceasefire, the Haji Pir Pass and other positions taken by 1 Para Bn. were returned to Pakistan. In June 1966 the battalion was sent to Gwalior, where it joined 7 and 8 Para Bns. in 51 Independent Para Bde.

Lt.Col. K. S. Pannu, commander of 2 Para Bde., 1971. Parachute wings are on the right shoulder, 50 Independent Para Brigade's formation sign on the left shoulder, jump indicator wings on the left pocket. The Parachute Regt. cap badge is pinned on the turban.

Between the Wars

During the 1965 war an *ad hoc* commando detachment composed of volunteers from various infantry units was organized by Lt. Col. Megh Singh of the Brigade of Guards. The detachment, dubbed 'Meghdoot Force', performed well in combat. In June 1966 the government authorized the Parachute Regt. to form a permanent commando unit. Known as 9 Bn., it was commanded by Lt.Col. Megh Singh, who used members of his Meghdoot Force as the nucleus.

In June 1967 elements of 9 Bn. were taken to form a second commando unit, 10 Bn., at Gwalior. During the following month both battalions left Gwalior: 9 Bn., which recruited primarily from northern peoples, operated with field units in the northern mountains; 10 Bn., which was drawn from Rajasthanis, was posted with units in the western desert. In 1969 these battalions were renamed 9 and 10 Para Commando Bns. respectively. Parachute and para commando battalions differed in one major respect: the former could be posted for tours in any part of India while para commando battalions develop a geographical specialization (i.e., desert or mountain warfare) and remain assigned to that sector.

Among the parachute battalions, 5 Para remained attached to

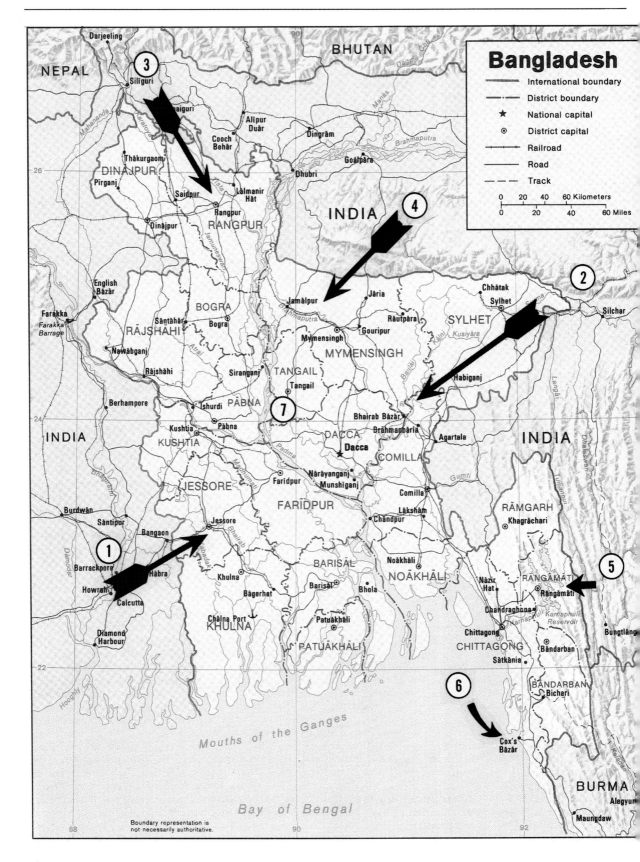

Bangladesh

————	International boundary
—·—·—	District boundary
★	National capital
⊙	District capital
┼┼┼┼	Railroad
————	Road
— — —	Track

0   20   40   60 Kilometers
0   20   40   60 Miles

Boundary representation is
not necessarily authoritative.

61 Mtn. Bde., but shifted from Nagaland to counter-insurgency operations in Mizoram. There the battalion faced harsh jungle operations against the rebel Mizo National Army, including long-range patrols and heliborne sweeps. In 17 months of operations in Mizoram casualties in the battalion were light; however, on 10 September 1967 a guerrilla ambush killed 12 paratroopers.

4 Para Bn. remained in Sikkim guarding the Chinese border for 39 months beginning in December 1965. In mid-1967 51 Independent Para Bde. moved its 7 and 8 Para Bns. to the Chinese border; the brigade was augmented by 3 Para in October.

In October 1969 2 Para Bn. rejoined 50 Independent Para Bde. after spending three tours in Kashmir; at the same time, 1 Para left the brigade to join 116 Inf. Bde. In April 1970 51 Independent Para Bde. began moving back from the border. Its 7 and 8 Para Bns. left the brigade in mid-year and joined 50 Independent Para Bde. at Agra; only 3 Para remained with 51 Independent Para Bde. 4 Para Bn., after its extended Sikkim tour, moved to Ambala to join 51 Independent Para Bde., while 5 Para left for the Chinese border.

THE 1971 WAR

In the 1965 Indo-Pakistan War action had focused on the western front; in 1971, attention was concentrated in the east. The origins of the conflict lay in growing Bengali nationalist sentiment in East Pakistan. By early March 1971 Bengalis organized a general strike; the East Pakistani authorities responded with a major crackdown by the armed forces and police on 25 March. Rebellion soon spread in East Pakistan; the Bengali nationalist guerrillas, known as 'Mukti Bahini', were trained and supported by India in a covert programme known as 'Operation Jackpot'. As the Mukti Bahini rapidly expanded, border clashes between East Pakistani and Indian forces also increased. By November 1971 constant border fighting made war appear all but inevitable.

To conduct a war in the east the Indian Army's Eastern Command had three corps surrounding East Pakistan: 2 Corps to the west, 4 Corps to the east, and 33 Corps to the north. The majority of the formations assigned to these corps were mountain divisions; because these divisions had to be returned quickly to their normal area of operations along the Chinese border, the Eastern Command realized that any war in East Pakistan had to be swift.

Although several mountain divisions were allotted for operations against East Pakistan, India still felt that it had fewer men than it needed to conduct offensive operations against the 42 regular battalions stationed in East Pakistan. For that reason Indian strategy involved containing Pakistani border strongpoints, then using mobile, flexible thrusts to cut Pakistani lines of communication and, finally, to race for Dacca.

During the 1971 War, Indian 2 Corps struck into East Pakistan from the south-west (1), 4 Corps from the north-east (2), 33 Corps from the north-west (3), and 101 Communications Zone from the north (4). 2 Para Bn. made its airborne jump at Tangail (7). The SFF infiltrated the Chittagong Hill Tracts (5), while an amphibious landing was made at Cox's Bazaar (6).

On the evening of 3 December 1971 with Indian forces massing along the border, the war opened with a series of pre-emptive Pakistani airstrikes into India. In the south-west sector 2 Corps began directing its offensive into East Pakistan from its headquarters in Krishnanagar, West Bengal. This corps was composed of 9 Inf. Div. and 4 Mtn. Div., which was already in West Bengal on internal security duties. Elements of 50 Independent Para Bde., still located in Calcutta after an internal security operation, were attached to the corps.

The initial target for 2 Corps was the town of Jessore. 4 Mtn. Div. was to operate north of the town, while 9 Inf. Div. was to take the town itself; 50 Independent Para Bde.'s 7 and 8 Para Bns. were initially tasked with assisting 9 Division. After Jessore fell quickly, however, the para brigade was ordered to cut the retreat of Pakistani soldiers north-east of Jessore. On 8 December the commander of 7 Para was killed while operating in the sector. Two days later the brigade (less 2 Para, which remained behind in East Pakistan) was airlifted to Delhi and deployed to the western theatre in the Punjab.

In the eastern sector, 4 Corps had been developing the infrastructure for a major offensive from Tripura since September. By mid-November the corps had readied three mountain divisions: 8 Mtn. Div., normally engaged in counter-insurgency in Nagaland; 23 Mtn. Div.; and 57 Mtn. Div., normally on counter-insurgency operations in Mizoram. In addition, three 'brigades' of Mukti Bahini were attached to the corps.

4 Corps was tasked with capturing all territory east of the Meghna River, and 8 Mtn. Div. with taking the town of Sylhet on the north-eastern border. Unfortunately the division was light and under strength, and had no experience in warfare other than counter-insurgency operations. On the morning of 8 December, after being given faulty information that the Pakistanis were withdrawing from Sylhet, the division conducted the first heliborne operation of the war when it landed one of its Gorkha battalions two kilometres from the town. The Pakistanis, however, had not retreated, and the Gorkhas were held at bay for five days before a relief column arrived. Sylhet was not taken by the division until 16 December, one day before the end of the war.

Some of the most spectacular operations of the war were conducted by 57 Mtn. Division. After moving swiftly to the east banks of the Meghna River, the corps commander approved a heliborne operation to cross the river south of the town of Bhairab Bazar. Significantly, both the 57 Mtn. Div. commander and the corps commander, himself a former commander of the same division, had conducted numerous heliborne operations while fighting rebels in Mizoram. On 9 December elements of the division's 311 Mtn. Bde. began their airmobile assault across the Meghna. Two days later the division's 73 Mtn. Bde. linked up after crossing the river in boats. 57 Mtn. Div. was now closing on Dacca fast.

To the south of 57 Div., 23 Mtn. Div. was assigned the Chandpur sector. By 9 December the division was able to push through the Pakistani defences and capture the town of Chandpur. Four days later the division's 301 Mtn. Bde. began crossing the Meghna in ferries.

In the north-west sector 33 Corps, headquartered in Shiliguri, was assigned 6 Mtn. Div., then on notice for possible operations in Bhutan, and 20 Mtn. Div.; in addition, the corps was allotted 71 Mtn. Bde. (later placed under the command of 6 Mtn. Div.) and 340 Mtn. Bde. Group. The initial thrust of this corps was towards the city of Rangpur.

From the Indian town of Shillong, north of East Pakistan, the Indians organized a mini-corps known as 101 Communications

Zone, composed of 95 Mtn. Bde. from Nagaland. On 8 December this zone was augmented with 167 Mtn. Brigade. The initial focus of this zone was the vicinity of Sherdpur.

By 10 December East Pakistan was being overwhelmed from all sides. To the north, 101 Communications Zone was pushing from Sherdpur toward the town of Tangail; to the west, 2 Corps was overrunning pockets of Pakistani defenders around Jessore; and to the east, 33 Corps was crossing the Meghna. Eager to end the war swiftly, Eastern Command decided to drop an airborne battalion to link up with 101 Communications Zone. On 11 December 2 Para Bn. was prepared for the drop at Tangail.

Their immediate mission was to seize the Poongli Bridge over the Lohajang River intact and intercept any Pakistanis retreating toward Dacca. At 1600 hours pathfinders from the battalion dropped from two C-119s. The rest of the battalion dropped from a fleet of C-47s, AN-12s, C-119s, and Caribous in 12-knot winds over the next hour. One soldier from the battalion was hung up by his parachute on the tail of the airplane for 20 min-

*Men from A Group, 10
Para Commando,
returning from the raid on
Islamkot, 16 December
1971.*

utes, but was able to drop to safety. The winds caused the battalion to spread; one stick even landed 20km from the intended dropzone. By 2000 hours, however, the bulk of the paratroopers were able to regroup and capture the Poongli Bridge intact. The paratroopers soon linked up with the flamboyant Mukti Bahini leader, Kader 'Tiger' Siddiqui. Together, they intercepted a battalion from the Pakistani 93 Bde.; the bulk of the withdrawing Pakistani brigade, however, had already escaped 2 Para's trap.

By the morning of 12 December the city of Dacca was faced with two Indian threats: to the north-west the paratroopers were consolidating their hold on Tangail; to the north-east 57 Mtn. Div. was awaiting armoured and infantry reinforcements before making the final push on Dacca.

On the night of 13/14 December 167 Mtn. Bde. from 101 Communications Zone linked up with 2 Para Bn. at Tangail; this reinforced combat group then began racing for Dacca. By the early morning of 16 December the head of the paratroop column was two miles from Dacca, and helped arrange a local ceasefire at 1100 hours. Thirty minutes later, both mountain brigades of 101 Communications Zone entered Dacca; elements of 57 Mtn. Div. reached Dacca's airport less than an hour later. The war in the east was over.

In the western theatre, fighting was largely divided between mountainous Kashmir and the desert sectors along the southern

The commander of 10 Para Commando, 1971. He wears the standard Indian Army parachute wing on the right shoulder, and 'Commando' tabs on both shoulders. A winged dagger, possibly an early Para Commando qualification insignia, is over the right pocket.

Battle and Theatre Honours, 1971

2 Para Bn:	Theatre Honours (East Pakistan)
	Battle Honours (Poongli Bridge)
9 Para Cdo:	Theatre Honours (Jammu and Kashmir)
10 Para Cdo:	Theatre Honours (Sindh)
	Battle Honours (Defence of Punch, and Chachro)
17 Para	
Field Regt:	Honour Title

half of the Indo-Pakistani border. In Kashmir 9 Para Cdo. Bn., which specialized in mountain warfare, had its baptism of fire. The battalion was divided into three groups, lettered A through C, each assigned to an infantry division. A Group, commanded by a major, was attached to 191 Inf. Bde. of 10 Inf. Div. in the Chhamb sector; the bulk of the group was used in a static defence role for the duration of the war. B Group, under 26 Inf. Div., saw limited action in the Jammu-Chhamb sector. C Group, attached to 25 Inf. Div., was tasked on the night of 13/14 December with destroying a Pakistani 122mm battery 12 miles south-west of the town of Punch. Splitting into seven assault teams, the group completed the mission at a cost of two dead and 14 wounded.

In the desert sector, 10 Para Cdo. Bn. was located at the outset of the war south-west of the town of Barmer in the Thar Desert of Rajasthan. The battalion's A and C Groups were tasked on 5 December with several shallow cross-border raids. During that night A Group's mission was cancelled, and both groups combined against C Group's target. On 14 December A Group moved to the Rann of Kutch and conducted a jeep raid on the Pakistani town of Islamkot. The ceasefire prevented any further raids from being launched.

Elsewhere in the western theatre, 1 Para Bn. was assigned to 116 Inf. Bde. in the Jalalabad sector. The battalion conducted several shallow cross-border operations, capturing some small Pakistani border posts. 51 Independent Para Bde. began the war in defensive positions in the northern sector of Rajasthan. With only two airborne battalions assigned (3 and 4 Para), the brigade was also allotted 11 Dogra Battalion. The brigade primarily defended the town of Ganganagar, although both parachute battalions conducted several limited raids. The brigade's biggest battle came on 28–29 December, well after the ceasefire, when 4 Para Bn. attempted to evict Pakistani troops from Indian soil; the battalion lost three company commanders in the process.

Both 5 and 6 Para Bns. sat out the war while tasked with patrolling the border with China.

Sikkim

In the immediate aftermath of the 1971 war, all battalions of the Parachute Regt. were given mixed companies; previously, parachute battalions had companies organized according to geographical or ethnic groups.

In 1974–75 the Indian Army decided to retain only a single parachute brigade. As a result, 51 Independent Para Bde. headquarters and support units reverted to non-airborne formations. 6, 7, and 8 Para Bns. were slated to be converted to infantry; however, only 8 Para was ultimately converted, becoming first 16 Mahar Bn., and later a mechanized battalion.

With only one parachute brigade remaining, three battalions were to be assigned to it at all times, while the other four battalions would be rotated through asssignments around the country. In addition, 9 Para Cdo. Bn. remained with Northern Command, while 10 Para Cdo. Bn. was in the desert under Western Command.

In early April 1975 the Indian Army moved to forcibly annex the independent mountain kingdom of Sikkim. With 17 Mtn. Div. in reserve, Indian army units moved into the city of Gangtok on 9 April. In the forefront was 1 Para Bn., which moved to disarm the Sikkimese Palace Guards. Sikkim was fully under Indian control within two days.

By the late 1970s, Indian paratroopers began training in High-Altitude Low-Opening (HALO) techniques. At the same time, 1 Para Bn. was selected for conversion into the army's third para commando battalion. Unlike its predecessors, 1 Para Cdo. Bn. was not given a geographic specialty, and was instead slated as the Parachute Regiment's 'strategic reserve'. 9 Para Cdo. Bn. remained an élite mountain unit co-located with Northern Command in the state of Jammu and Kashmir; 10 Para Cdo. Bn., a desert unit, was with Western Command. In the mid-1980s there was discussion of bringing the three para commando battalions together under a new Special Forces Regiment; these plans were shelved, and the para commandos continue to be trained and recruited by the Parachute Regiment.

Formation insignia for the 8 Mountain Division (left)—yellow 8, red bayonet, on black; and 57 Mountain Division (right)—white crossed weapons, red motif with yellow and black details, on black.

Operation 'Bluestar'

In early 1984 anti-government violence by Sikh terrorists in the state of Punjab had grown to alarming proportions. Preparing for a major crackdown against terrorism, the government made plans to mass six divisions in the Punjab. Among these were 4 and 23 Mtn. Divs., and 54 Div., a general reserve unit.

By the end of May the government had made the decision to move against the terrorists. On the night of 30 May 9 Inf. Div. began moving from its base at Meerut to the city of Amritsar, a key Sikh holy city in the Punjab. On the night of 1 June a curfew was declared in Amritsar; two days later, the state was sealed by army units.

The focus of the battle in Amritsar was to be the Golden Temple, an extensive complex of stone buildings which had been effectively fortified by Sikh extremists. After surrounding the temple, the army began Operation 'Bluestar'—the capture of the Golden Temple—by lightly shelling the Sikh positions on 4 June. Highly motivated and well-armed, the Sikhs were unshaken by the bombardment. After softening up the defenders for another day, the army decided to launch a ground assault on the night of 5 June. The first attempt was made by paramilitary commandos from the Special Frontier Forces. This having failed, the army took over on the same night.

Leading the army's charge were elements of 1 Para Cdo. Battalion. Dressed in black dungarees and bullet-proof vests, 40 commandos infiltrated the temple to evacuate several moderate Sikh leaders. They immediately faced withering machine-gun fire. Four prominent Sikhs were successfully exfiltrated; two were shot and killed. In addition, the commandos suffered three killed and 19 wounded.

The commandos were then assigned to lead infantry assault groups back into the temple. Storming the Sikh machine-gun emplacements, the commandos took heavy casualties; of the 80 men committed, half were wounded and 14 killed. After gaining a foothold in the temple, infantry units, tanks, and artillery pounded the terrorist positions over the next day. Sikh resistance crumbled, and it was then up to the commandos to comb tunnels and basements to root out the remaining terrorists. One week later, during a visit to the temple by Indian President Zail Singh,

the commandos suffered their final casualty at the Golden Temple: the commander of 1 Para Cdo. Bn. was hit in the upper arm by a sniper while standing a few feet from the president.

Air Assault

In 1985 Gen. K. Sundarji, the chief of Army Staff, approved plans to convert 54 Inf. Div. into 54 Air Assault Division. The division, based in Hyderabad/Secunderabad, had long been one of the army's strategic reserve formations, of which the Indian Army normally maintains three, and sometimes four. 54 Div. was unique in that during 1981–82 one of its brigades was given some training in amphibious operations. Another, 47 Inf. Bde., was given some light airmobile training when it was flown from Hyderabad to Delhi during Operation 'Trident' in late January 1987. Because of insufficient helicopter assets, however, the division's 'air assault' designation meant in reality only that it was adept at quickly loading and unloading from transport aircraft.

In the winter of 1986–87 India launched a massive military exercise, codenamed 'Brasstacks', in the desert regions along the Indo–Pakistani border. The exercise, the largest in Indian history, involved elements of 13 divisions, many of them located in the west ever since heavy communal fighting had broken out following the assassination of Prime Minister Indira Gandhi in late 1984. Among the formations used in 'Brasstacks' were elements of 4 Mtn., 57 Mtn., 23 Mtn. and 54 Air Assault Divisions.

Sri Lanka

In May 1987 the Sri Lankan army began a major ground and air campaign against Tamil rebels concentrated in the Jaffna Peninsula in the north of the country. The Indian government, which faced growing discontent among its own southern Tamil population, began to pressure Colombo to cease its offensive. As part of these pressure tactics, 10 Para Cdo. Bn. embarked on an Indian Navy task force on 21 July. On the following day the task force steamed off the horizon of Colombo, sending a clear signal to the Sri Lankan government.

On 29 July 1987 India and Sri Lanka signed an accord whereby an Indian Peace-keeping Force (IPKF) would be sent to Sri Lanka to engineer the disarming of Tamil guerrillas in the northern province of the country and oversee a ceasefire. On the same day, the para commandos in the Indian task force were landed at Colombo harbour in order to provide security during the signing of the accord.

As India's designated rapid deployment unit, 54 Air Assault Div. was selected as the core of the IPKF. One of the division's brigades, 76 Inf., had already moved by rail to Madras as part of India's pressure tactics against the Sri Lankan government. On 30 July the initial elements of the division began landing at Jaffna airfield in northern Sri Lanka. By the end of August all three of the division's brigades were in Sri Lanka, though all at less than half strength. Two battalions of 91 Inf. Bde. were on the north-western corner of the Jaffna Peninsula, while a third battalion was stationed inside Jaffna City. 47 Inf. Bde. was at Vavuniya, south of Jaffna, and 76 Inf. Bde. at Batticaloa on the eastern coast. In addition, 340 Independent Bde., which had been training in amphibious operations since 1983, was landed at Trincomalee, the major port in eastern Sri Lanka. Also assigned to the IPKF was 10 Para Cdo. Bn., which had moved north from Colombo.

By early October, relations had become strained between the IPKF and the Tamil Tiger guerrillas. Fighting became all but inevitable after five commandos were kidnapped by the Tamils and brutally murdered. In order to cripple the Tamil guerrilla network, the Indian Army planned to capture the insurgent headquarters in Jaffna City. To reinforce the lone brigade of 54 Air Assault Div. on Jaffna, two brigades from 36 Inf. Div. were flown to Jaffna and placed under the operational control of 54 Division. Codenamed Operation 'Pawan', the Indian plan involved an initial heliborne assault into the centre of the city followed by a multi-prong ground advance from all directions.

The initial heliborne assault involved a company of 10 Para Cdo. Bn. acting as pathfinders. Boarding Mi-8 choppers on 11 October, the commandos flew in low over Jaffna City. Unaware that their radio communications were being monitored by the Tamils, the commandos landed in a soccer field and were immediately pinned down by heavy machine gun fire: two helicopters were damaged and six commandos killed instantly. A second wave of choppers containing a platoon from 13 Sikh Light Infantry came under more intense fire, making further reinforcements impossible: all but one of the Sikhs perished. Cornered and running out of ammunition, the commandos pleaded for reinforcements. Their battalion commander, Lt.Col. Dalbir Singh, personally led a column of T-72 tanks the next morning to relieve his beleaguered men.

After the failure of the commando assault, the infantry brigades slowly fought their way into Jaffna City over the next 16 days. Because of heavy Tamil resistance, two more brigades were rushed to Jaffna before the end of the battle. The entire operation was marked by major confusion on the part of the IPKF. 5 Para Bn., for example, was initially placed under the command of 18 Inf. Bde., then shifted to 72 Inf. Bde., then back to 18 Brigade: as a result, neither brigade was able to maximize the use of this battalion.

By the end of November, Jaffna was completely in IPKF hands. Most of the Tamil guerrillas, however, had slipped out of the Indian net and exfiltrated to the east. With their duties fast becoming a protracted affair, the IPKF shifted 36 Inf. Div. to handle counter-insurgency operations in the Eastern Province. The Northern Province, meanwhile, remained 54 Air Assault Div.'s area of operations.

After their failed assault into Jaffna City, 10 Para Cdo. Bn. was used in November for a heliborne assault in the town of Moolai 14 miles to the north-west. Twenty-five guerrillas were killed and an arms depot seized. In December 5 Para Bn., still assigned to 18 Inf. Bde., lost six men to a Tamil landmine. Assigned to infantry divisions, parachute battalions rotated regularly through the IPKF for the duration of the war.

By January 1988 the IPKF included the entire 54 Air Assault and 36 Inf. Div., two brigades of 4 Mtn. Div., and several other independent brigades and support units. By February the entire 57 Mtn. Div., long experienced in counter-insurgency, had arrived in Sri Lanka and was used on a major sweep in the vicinity of Batticaloa. To provide increased firepower and mobility, infantry battalions formed platoon-sized Quick Reaction Teams (QRTs) as mobile strike forces.

In order to give the commandos battle experience, 10 Para Cdo. Bn. was rotated home in early 1988 and replaced by 9 Para Cdo. Battalion. 9 Para Cdo., in turn, was scheduled to return in June, but had its tour extended for an air assault into the coastal swamps around Mullaittivu. There the battalion participated in a multi-battalion sweep that located several arms caches. During its

Members of 9 Para Commando aboard a transport aircraft in Sri Lanka, 1988. Headgear includes maroon berets, knit caps, and black bandanas. Commandos on the right hold Indian-made copies of the FN FAL; the soldier in the left foreground an AK-47. India allegedly purchased several thousand AK-47s from Poland for use by élite units in Sri Lanka. (Courtesy India Today)

tour 9 Para Cdo. Bn. also provided 12 men for security around the Indian High Commission in Colombo.

In March 1989 the IPKF launched Operation 'Bazz' ('Falcon'), a clearing drive in the east involving mountain troops and paratroopers. Two months later the IPKF withdrew 8,000 of its 50,000 men to India; included in this first contingent was a para commando battalion. Still stationed in Sri Lanka was the 57 Mtn. Div. in Batticaloa; 4 Mtn. Div. in the Vavuniya sector; 54 Air Assault Div. in Jaffna; and 36 Inf. Div. in Trincomalce.

In July 1989 the IPKF launched Operation 'Toofan' ('Storm') in the east. Some 500 recently arrived para commandos were allegedly involved.

Over the next few months, the IPKF was considerably reduced in size. On 31 March 1990 the final 2,000 men of the IPKF were sent home; among these were at least one airborne battalion. In 30 months the Indians had lost 1,115 dead in Sri Lanka; worse, they had failed to achieve peace in that troubled nation.

In the immediate aftermath of the Sri Lankan operation the Indian Army pondered what to do with the IPKF, which in size and mission had become effectively a new 'corps'. Because ten-

sions were heating up along the Pakistani border in Kashmir, the IPKF framework was converted into the new 21 Corps and deployed to Kashmir in early 1990. The corps headquarters is rumoured to be in Bhopal, central India, but it will be available for deployment to trouble spots around the country. 57 Mtn. Div., which returned from Sri Lanka in January 1990, was placed under 21 Corps and sent to the Kashmir border. In addition, the bulk of 8 Mtn. Division was shifted from counter-insurgency in the east to the new corps. Finally, the corps was allotted elements of 23 Mtn. Div. normally held in reserve in Ranchi, and of 21

Mtn. Div., usually deployed along the Sikkim-Bhutan border.

Also in the aftermath of the IPKF, the Indian Army recognized that it lacked the helicopter assets to make 54 Air Assault Div. a truly airmobile formation. At best, selected elements of the division were able to conduct heliborne training exercises twice a year. Because of this deficiency the division was once again designated 54 Inf. Division.

The Maldives

At 0415 hours on 3 November 1988, 150 Sri Lankan mercenaries landed in two trawlers off the Maldives, an island nation off the coast of south-western India. Using machine guns, rockets, and grenades, the mercenaries entered Male, the capital, and attacked the president's residence and the headquarters of the Maldivian militia. After receiving a call for assistance from the Maldivian president, the Indian cabinet approved the dispatch of military units at 1530 on 3 November. Selected for the task was 50 Independent Para Brigade. Six hours after cabinet approval, the paratroopers launched the Maldives operation, codenamed 'Cactus'.

In the initial two Il-76 transports leaving Agra were elements of 6 Para Bn. and 17 Para Field Regt., the airborne brigade's heavy weapons unit. In the lead aircraft was Brig. F. F. C. Bulsara, the brigade commander, and the Indian High Commissioner to the Maldives, who was in Delhi at the time of the attempted coup. Flying four hours non-stop to the Maldives, the aircraft approached Hulule Airport, located on an island three kilometres

Paratroopers on the last ship departing Sri Lanka, March 1990. (Courtesy India Today*)*

**Order of Battle
Indian Peace-Keeping Force
October 1987**

54 Air Assault Div.	
91 Inf. Bde.	Jaffna
5 Madras Bn.	
8 Mahar Bn.	
1 Mahratta LI Bn.	
76 Inf. Bde.	Mannar-Vavuniya-Mulliativu
47 Inf. Bde.	Trincomalee-Batticoloa-Amparai
36 Inf. Div.	
115 Inf. Bde.	Jaffna
72 Inf. Bde.	Jaffna
4 Bn./5 Gorkha Regt.	
13 Sikh LI Bn.	
41 Inf. Bde.	Jaffna
5 Rajputana Rifles	
18 Inf. Bde.	Jaffna
5 Para Bn.	
Independent	
340 Independent Bde.	Trincomalee
10 Para Cdo. Bn.	Jaffna
65 Armd. Regt. (elements)	Jaffna

*Paratroopers armed with
FN FALs board an Il-76
transport.*

from Male. The paratroopers made an uncontested landing and established control around the airfield in 30 minutes.

Commandeering local boats, two platoons from 6 Para crossed to Male. By 0230 on 4 November the Maldivian president was located and escorted to safety. The paratroopers then spread throughout the city unopposed, the mercenaries having previously fled. At the same time, a ship was seen fleeing Male, and it was discovered that mercenaries were on board with hostages, including the Maldivian Minister of Education. The commander of 17 Para Field Regt. rushed machine guns and rocket launchers to the southern tip of the island and fired on the ship. Though hit, the vessel escaped, only to be stopped and boarded by Indian naval forces the following day.

On the morning of 4 November, a fleet of Il-76s, An-12s, and An-32s flew in the remainder of 6 Para Bn. and 10 Para Cdo. Bn.; later that morning 10 Para Cdo. were flown by Mi-8 choppers to the outlying islands to search for escaping mercenaries.

Operation 'Cactus' concluded without any casualties among the paratroopers. Elements of 6 Para remained in the Maldives to provide protection for exactly one year after the failed coup attempt.

Amphibious Operations

India's first amphibious operation took place during the 1971 war. In order to prevent East Pakistani forces from retreating east into Burma, the Indian Army planned to capture the coastal town of Cox's Bazaar. Assigned to the operation was Romeo Force, an *ad hoc* headquarters controlling a Gorkha battalion, elements of a Bihari battalion, and artillery.

Romeo Force assembled in Calcutta on the night of 10/11 December 1971 and set sail aboard the merchant ship *Vishva Vijay* at 0445 hours on 12 December. On the night of 13/14 December the force transferred to two landing ships and veered toward the coast. Because of unfavourable tidal conditions they waited until the following night before making the final assault. Sandbars, however, prevented the ships from beaching. Several troops attempted to wade ashore, but two Gorkhas drowned. The operation was immediately halted. Later on 15 December, the force, sitting vulnerably offshore, transferred to local boats and landed over the next day. They found no resistance at Cox's Bazaar.

In the early 1980s the Indian Army began conducting amphibious training exercises. In 1981 a brigade from 54 Inf. Div. made an amphibious landing at Port Blair in the Andaman Island chain; Prime Minister Indira Gandhi attended the exercise. During the following year a brigade from the same division again conducted an amphibious landing at Port Blair. In 1983, however, 340 Independent Bde. based at Trivandrum was designated as the army's amphibious formation and began conducting the annual landings in the Andamans. Its three battalions are generally chosen from the army's southern-based regiments. In early 1986 the brigade, supported by paratroopers, conducted an amphibious/airmobile training exercise codenamed 'Tri Shakti' off the coast of Goa. This brigade was among the first units to arrive in Sri Lanka as part of the IPKF, where it remained at the port of Trincomalee for virtually the entire duration of the IPKF's existence.

Indian Marine Special Forces

During the early 1950s the Indian Navy sent students to England for scuba training. In 1955 the Navy established its own diving school at Cochin. By the mid-1960s sufficient divers had been trained at Cochin to form two detachments, one for the western fleet at Bombay, and one for the eastern fleet at Vishakhapatam. These diver detachments performed clearance, salvage, and underwater demolitions assignments.

During the 1971 war Navy divers saw heavy action while training underwater sappers in the Mukti Bahini. Indian divers themselves led most of the sabotage operations into East Pakistani ports.

In 1984, divers from Bombay were sent to the Golden Temple to retrieve weapons hidden in the temple's extensive reflecting pools.

In 1986 the Indian Navy began forming a naval commando unit based on the US Navy SEAL Teams. This unit would be used for special operations, as well as for protecting India's offshore oil rigs. In February 1987 the Navy formally established the Indian Marine Special Forces (IMSF). The unit's provisional commander, Lt. Arvind Singh, and one other officer had just completed training at Coronado, California, with the US SEALs.

It was not until 11 October 1987 that the unit received its baptism of fire. On that day Lt. Singh accompanied army comman-

Men of 6 Para Bn. at the headquarters of the National Security Service, *Maldives, November 1988. (Courtesy India Today)*

dos on the ill-fated heliborne assault into Jaffna City. Navy commandos also helped clear the Navanturai Coastal Road west of Jaffna City to allow a linkup with the advancing 41 Infantry Brigade.

On the night of 21 October 18 IMSF commandos, including Lt. Singh, boarded two Gemini rafts off the coast of Jaffna City and towed two wooden rafts of explosives into a channel leading to the city's Guru Nagar Jetty. Avoiding mines, eight men and two officers shifted to the wooden rafts and paddled to the jetty, then fixed demolition charges to the jetty and Tamil speedboats. The commandos were detected, but laid down suppressive fire and detonated the explosives before retreating to the Geminis without taking casualties. Two nights later, commandos swam back into the harbour to destroy the remaining speedboats. They were again detected, and sustained minor injuries. For leading

these actions, the 30-year-old Lt. Singh became the youngest officer to receive the Maha Vir Chakra Award.

In November 1988 the IMSF again saw action when it was called upon to board a hijacked vessel containing Sri Lankan mercenaries and several hostages, including the Maldivian Minister of Education. The IMSF boarded the vessel, though after the mercenaries had announced their surrender to Indian authorities.

By 1991 the IMSF, based in Bombay, had expanded to 300 men, commanded by a commodore. All IMSF personnel are airborne-qualified at Agra and diver-qualified at Cochin.

Paramilitary Units

Several élite commando and intelligence formations come under the Director General for Security, who is answerable to the Indian Prime Minister. These include the Research and Analysis Wing (RAW), India's external intelligence agency; the Special Frontier Force; the Aviation Research Centre; the National Security Guard; the Special Protection Group; and the Special Security Bureau, which raised militias along the Chinese frontier.

Lt. Arvind Singh, provisional commander of the IMSF, receives the Maha Vir Chakra Award from the Indian President for his October 1987 actions in Sri Lanka. (Courtesy India Today)

Indian Marine Special Forces formation sign (top)—white letters and ring inside yellow/black cable, all on maroon; and combat diver qualification insignia (bottom), in yellow metal.

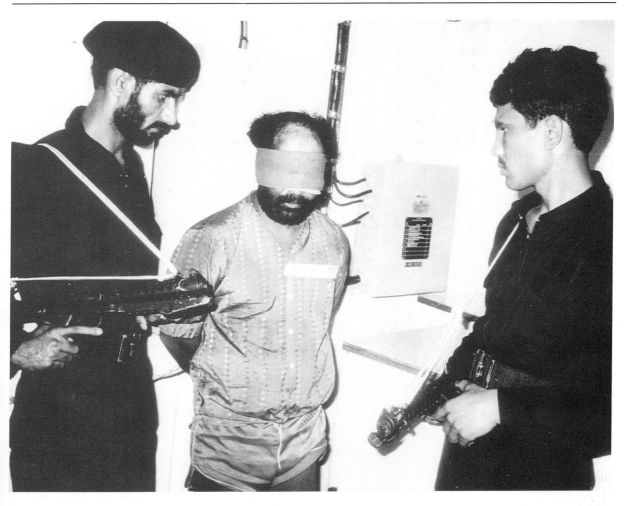

In practice, the Director General for Security and the director of the RAW are usually the same person.

Special Frontier Force

On 14 November 1962 near the end of the Sino-Indian War, the Nehru government ordered the raising of an élite guerrilla force composed of Tibetan refugees then living in India. The unit was to be parachuted behind Chinese lines in the event of another war along the Tibetan frontier. Established under the direct supervision of the Prime Minister, the new outfit was named the Special Frontier Force. A retired Indian army major-general was made Inspector General of the new formation; he was renowned for his unconventional thinking and had been, among other assignments, commander of 22 Mtn. Regt. during World War Two. Taking the number from this wartime unit, the SFF soon became known by the codename 'Establishment 22'.

The SFF made its base at Chakrata, a mountain town in the foothills of the Himalayas 100 kilometres from the large Tibetan refugee population in the city of Dehra Dun. With an initial strength of 12,000 men, the Force began six months of training in rock-climbing and guerrilla warfare. Advisors were brought in from the US and the Indian Army. The unit's weapons, all provided by the US, consisted of M-1s, M-2s, and M-3s. No heavy weapons were provided to the unit.

IMSF commandos guard the mercenary commander after boarding the hijacked ship in the Maldives, 1988. The commandos wear black fatigues and dark blue berets. (Courtesy India Today)

The Tibetans proved to be excellent guerrilla warriors. By late 1963, however, inter-service rivalry led to severe criticism of the SFF by the regular army. To prove the unit's worth in unconventional warfare, the Inspector General despatched 120 of his Tibetans for a field exercise, codenamed 'Garuda', against a regular Army brigade in the hills around Simla. After they had been pinned down for three days by the SFF guerrillas, the Army was less inclined to criticise.

In 1964 the SFF unsuccessfully requested the Army to provide airborne training. After appealing directly to the Prime Minister, the entire force, led by the Inspector General, was allowed to complete six jumps at Agra. The SFF then began its own airborne training programme at Sarasawan Airbase near Saharanpur.

By the late 1960s the 12,000-strong SFF was organized into six battalions for administrative purposes. Each battalion, consisting of six companies, was commanded by the Tibetan equivalent of a lieutenant-colonel. A Tibetan major or captain commanded each company, which was the primary unit used in operations. In ad-

6 Para Battalion in the Maldives. Weapons include the Sterling and the Indian-made 7.62mm FAL. (Courtesy India Today)

dition, there were two female signal and medical companies. During this time the SFF was never used on guerrilla operations against its intended enemy, China. However, the unit did conduct limited cross-border reconnaissance operations, as well as highly classified forays to place sensors in the Himalayas to detect Chinese nuclear and missile tests.

It was not until 1971 that the SFF was used in major combat. With the Inspector General temporarily assigned to training Bangladeshi insurgents, seven companies of the SFF were being used for traffic control at Ladakh. The Inspector General protested this misuse of his unit to the Prime Minister, and asked that the SFF be used against East Pakistan; permission was granted, and in late October elements were ordered to Mizoram.

By November approximately one-third of the 9,000-strong SFF was deployed adjacent to the Chittagong Hill Tracts. Cross-border attacks were becoming more frequent, and the SFF was instructed late in the month to begin raids into the Chittagong Hill Tracts. For the operation, codenamed 'Eagle', the SFF was equipped with US carbines and Bulgarian AK-47s. In addition, the first Dapon, the Tibetan equivalent of a brigadier, was selected to command part of the SFF task force.

With war fast approaching, the SFF was given several mission plans, including the destruction of the Kaptai Dam and other bridges. The Inspector General urged that his men be used to capture Chittagong, but this was vetoed because the Tibetans were not assigned artillery or airlift support.

After 21 days of border fighting the SFF divided its six battalions into three columns and moved into East Pakistan by 3 December. After capturing several towns in the Chittagong Hill Tracts the Tibetans were given some mortars and recoilless rifles; in addition, they were allotted two Mi-4 helicopters. By the time the ceasefire was declared on 17 December, the SFF had lost 56 killed and nearly 190 wounded. The force was able to block a potential escape route for East Pakistani forces into Burma. In addition, they pinned down elements of the Pakistani 97 Independent Bde. and 2 Cdo. Bn. in the Chittagong Hill Tracts.

In the immediate aftermath of the war 580 men from the Force were awarded cash prizes by the Indian government for their involvement. Many Tibetan political leaders, however, were extremely critical of the use of the SFF against anybody but a Chinese enemy.

In 1973 the original Indian Inspector General of the SFF was replaced. Two years later a new rule was issued prohibiting the unit from being deployed within 10 kilometres of the Chinese border. This came about after several incidents in which overzealous Tibetan commandos had engaged in unsanctioned cross-border operations. In 1968, for example, elements of the Force crossed into China three times, killing three Chinese with no losses. In 1971 SFF units in Ladakh had a four-hour firefight with Chinese forces, resulting in two Tibetans killed.

By the late 1970s the future of the SFF was no longer certain. With Indo-Chinese tensions easing somewhat, there was criticism of the maintenance of a Tibetan commando force as an unnecessary expense. However, the SFF was soon given a new mission: counter-terrorism. Because the Tibetans were foreign-

SFF silver metal cap badge.

ers, and therefore not directly involved in Indian communal politics, they were seen as an ideal, objective counter-terrorist force. As a result, in 1977 the Director General for Security ordered 500 SFF commandos to deploy to Sarasawa for possible action against rioters during national elections. After the elections were conducted without major incident only 60 Tibetans were retained at Sarasawa for counter-terrorist duties. However, over 500 men selected from throughout the Army were sent to Sarasawa for counter-terrorist training. This new élite detachment, known as the Special Group, falls under the control of the SFF Inspector General.

Significantly, all Tibetans were removed from the Special Group and returned to Chakrata. Among the Tibetan members of the SFF, three commando battalions were raised for deployment around the country; one of these battalions is normally stationed on the Siachen Glacier. The remainder of the SFF was still configured for guerrilla operations in China.

By early 1984 the SFF's Special Group was the nation's primary counter-terrorist force. When it became clear in the late spring that an assault on the Sikh Golden Temple might be necessary, the detachment practised attacks on a mockup of the temple near Sarasawa. In June 1984 a squad from the Special Group was dispatched to the Golden Temple. On the night of 5 June these commandos conducted the first assault on the temple, entering from a back alley and storming it from the rear. They soon became pinned down, however, and were quickly withdrawn.

IMSF commandos at their training centre in Bombay, September 1988. They are dressed in black with black helmets. The weapon is the Mk 4 Sterling. The IMSF insignia is visible on the right shoulder. Parachute wings are worn on the right breast by the man on the left. (Courtesy India Today)

An SFF guerrilla team in the Chittagong Hill Tracts during the 1971 War. They are armed with AK-47s procured from Bulgaria.

In late 1984 the Special Group was temporarily used for VIP security around the Prime Minister following the assassination of Indira Gandhi.

Currently, one SFF battalion is normally kept in the extreme north-west on the Siachen Glacier. In 1985–86 several members of the Force were given bravery medals for their actions on the glacier. Total SFF strength currently fluctuates between 8,000 and 10,000 men. Battalions remain composed of six companies, each company consisting of 123 men. In 1989 there were 64 purely Tibetan companies; the remaining men were recruited primarily from among hill tribes in the vicinity of Chakrata. In addition, there is a limit of 700 Gorkhas allowed into the SFF at any one time.

Training, conducted at Chakrata, lasts six months and is identical to basic Indian Army training, with additional instruction in rock-climbing and guerrilla tactics. All members are parachute qualified at Sarasawan after five jumps from an AN-12, with three refresher jumps every year. Twelve US parachute instructors remained until 1968.

SFF commandos previously wore the SFF formation insignia on the left breast; it is now worn on the shoulder. Unique SFF parachute wings were worn on the left shoulder; since the mid-1970s, however, the standard Indian Army parachute wing has been worn on the right breast. An airborne maroon beret is worn with a distinctive SFF beret badge and an SFF tab is worn on both shoulders. In 1989 the SFF began wearing standard Indian DPM camouflage.

Aviation Research Centre

The Aviation Research Centre (ARC) is the élite airlift wing controlled by Indian intelligence. Raised in 1963, the ARC initially consisted of C-46 transports, Helio STOL aircraft, and U-5 twin-Helio STOL aircraft. All pilots were seconded from the Air Force. The ARC was responsible largely for the parachute training and transportation of the SFF. It also conducted limited aerial reconnaissance of the Pakistani and Chinese borders. It was additionally assigned politically sensitive missions, such as transporting the Tibetan Dalai Lama from Delhi during heavy rioting in late 1984. In the 1980s the ARC was equipped primarily with An-12s and An-32s. In addition, there are four light aircraft for VIP liaison. There was some discussion of obtaining the C-130 for the ARC, but these plans have apparently been shelved.

Special Protection Group

In March 1985 the Home Ministry created the Special Protection Group (SPG) as an élite security detail to guard the Prime Minister and his family. Patterned after the US Secret Service, the SPG consisted of 1,500 police marksmen and bodyguards. During an assassination attempt on Prime Minister Rajiv Gandhi in October 1986 the SPG was criticized for its slow response. In December 1989 the new Indian Prime Minister, V. P. Singh, suggested cutting back on the size of the SPG. The Group, however, remains in force as of 1991.

National Security Guard

In 1984 the Indian Home Ministry began forming an élite commando force to deal with counter-terrorism and hostage rescues.

Patterned after the German GSG-9 and in consultation with the British SAS, the new force was called the National Security Guard (NSG). Because of their black uniforms, they were soon dubbed the 'Black Cats'.

The NSG was divided into two formations: the 4,000-man Special Action Group (SAG), composed of Army personnel initially seconded mainly from the Parachute Regiment; and 2,300 Special Ranger Group (SRG), seconded from other paramilitary units. The SAG was composed of 300-man battalions, each divided into three squadrons. NSG headquarters was at Gurgaon, on the outskirts of Delhi.

Although they were not intended for VIP security, NSG commandos were soon providing protection for a growing number of politicians. Aside from this misuse, the NSG also came under criticism for its unusually high proportion of officers and its extravagant budget.

SFF radio operators pose during the 1971 war. Note the US-supplied M-1 Garand in the centre background.

NSG insignia: the early formation insignia (left) features a yellow-flaming red circular blade balanced on a finger, the finger of a pink and white hand; according to Hindu legend, the flying blade could decapitate victims. The cap badge (right) is gold bullion with red and black details and a red on white scroll. Both backgrounds are black.

Tibetan Dapon (brigadier) from the Special Frontier Force, 1978. He wears a maroon beret with the SFF cap badge; the same badge is seen on the belt buckle. On his left shoulder is the SFF formation insignia; an SFF title is worn on both shoulders. The rank insignia are of a design unique to the SFF. Standard Indian Army parachute wings are worn over the right pocket; in the mid-1970s the SFF's distinctive 'flying dagger' parachute wings were phased out. A small jump indicator wing is pinned to the left pocket.

Tibetan SFF commandos, early 1970s; they wear parachute crash helmets and are armed with the Indian Mk 4 Sterling. SFF formation insignia are worn on the left shoulder, the SFF's unique 'flying dagger' parachute wings on the right shoulder.

On 30 April 1986 NSG commandos stormed the Golden Temple in Operation 'Black Thunder'. Compared to Operation 'Bluestar' in 1984, however, this was a tame affair: no weapons were discovered and nobody was killed.

In late 1987 the NSG was airlifted to Andhra Pradesh after government hostages were taken by a Marxist group. Before the Black Cats could be used in their proper role, however, the hostages were released.

In May 1988 the NSG launched Operation 'Black Thunder II', their largest operation to date, prompted by increased terrorist activity from within the Golden Temple. The Black Cats planned the storming of the temple for three months. On 9 May, after a police inspector general was shot outside the temple, the NSG was ordered to move.

By 12 May, 1,000 NSG commandos had arrived at the temple. Black Cat sniper teams armed with the Heckler & Koch PSG-1 rifle with night scope took up positions, including atop a 300-foot watertower. While commandos from the 51 SAG divided into assault squadrons, Ranger Groups were used to seal off the area around the temple and for tactical support. On 15 May the NSG

began its attack. Machine gun fire and rockets were used to cut holes in the temple's minarets, followed by teargas canisters. Once it was determined that the towers had been abandoned, the SAG used explosives to break holes into the temple basement. By 18 May all militants had surrendered at the cost of only two wounded Black Cats.

In mid-1990 an NSG battalion was again deployed to the Punjab to confront Sikh rioters. There they began training the Punjabi police in counter-terrorism. Currently, the Army continues to loan personnel to the SAG, although most tend to come from units other than the Parachute Regiment. One SAG team is permanently stationed at Indira Gandhi International Airport in New Delhi for hostage situations.

Indo-Tibetan Border Police

Established at a strength of twenty companies in the immediate aftermath of the 1962 war, the Indo-Tibetan Border Police (ITBP) is tasked with patrolling the Chinese frontier. At the instigation of several flamboyant commanders in the 1970s, ITBP personnel were given martial arts training and several élite ski detachments were raised. In addition, commando units of the ITBP were being used for VIP protection around the Prime Minister at the time Indira Gandhi was assassinated in 1984.

In 1990 the ITBP had 120 companies each with 85 men. They are occasionally used for VIP security, and have seen limited action on counter-terrorist operations in the Punjab in the late 1980s.

PAKISTAN: ARMY AIRBORNE

Following the partition of India and Pakistan in August 1947, the British-raised 2 Indian Abn. Div. was divided between the two countries. Of the division's three brigades, Pakistan was given the headquarters of 14 Para Bde.; the para battalions, however, did not remain attached to the division's headquarters or brigades – rather, each battalion returned to its original pre-airborne regiment. Thus five of the division's 11 para battalions followed their parent regiments back to Pakistan:

2 Airborne Division

Designation	Parent Regiment
3 Bn./Division HQ	15 Punjab Regt.
1 Bn./14 Para Bde.	Frontier Force Regt.
3 Bn./14 Para Bde.	16 Punjab Regt.
3 Bn./50 Para Bde.	1 Punjab Regt.
3 Bn./50 Para Bde.[1]	The Baluch Regt.

No battalions from 77 Para Bde. went to Pakistan. However, Pakistan did receive the former British Parachute School at Chaklala.

In the confusing months immediately after partition, 14 Para Bde., bolstered by non-airborne units, was stationed in Sialkot. By late 1947 Pakistan was fighting with India over control of territory in Jammu and Kashmir and elements of the parachute brigade were used in the ground role. Soon afterwards all airborne training for the unit stopped, although the brigade retained its 'parachute' designation. To this day the parachute brigade is still assigned to the Sialkot sector. Just as with the rest of the Pakistan Army, battalions assigned to 14 Para Bde. are rotated every two or three years.

In 1953–54 the Pakistan Army raised an élite commando formation with US Army assistance. To disguise its true mission the new unit was simply designated 19 Bn. of the Baluch Regiment. The battalion was posted to a new headquarters at Cherat near Attock City.

19 Baluch saw its first action during the mid-1950s in East Pakistan while training Naga rebels fighting against the Indian government. The Naga rebellion began in 1954 and was to remain an irritant through the early 1970s.

In March 1964 a Mobile Training Team from the US Army 10 Special Forces Group (Airborne) went to Pakistan to set up a new airborne school at Peshawar for 19 Baluch; the school included basic and jumpmaster courses. All members of 19 Baluch were airborne-qualified with five jumps. The training team also included four riggers, who helped train Pakistani counterparts.

By this time, members of 19 Baluch were already referring to themselves as the 'Special Service Group' (SSG) of The Baluch Regiment. The battalion at the time was commanded by a colonel and numbered 700 men. It was divided into 24 'companies', some with only a dozen men. Each company had a specialization, including desert, mountain, ranger, and underwater warfare. The desert companies participated in training exercises with a US Army SF Mobile Training Team in late 1964. The scuba company at Karachi was renowned for its tough physical training and poor equipment maintenance.

(1) There were two '3 Para Battalions' in 50 Para Bde., distinguished by their different parent regiments.

Members of the National Security Guard's Special Ranger Group, January 1991. They wear black uniforms with black berets and yellow on maroon 'Ranger' tabs on both shoulders. On the left shoulder the current NSG formation insignia, featuring the head of a black cat, would also be worn.

The 1965 War

Not until the September 1965 Indo-Pakistan War did the battalion see its first combat. The Pakistani commandos were tasked with a series of ambitious parachute raids to paralyse three forward Indian airbases at Pathankot, Adampur, and Halwara. They intended to coordinate their attacks with Pakistani airstrikes on the bases. On completion of their mission the commandos were to be exfiltrated by aircraft or, failing this, to escape and evade back to the Pakistani border.

On the night of 7 September the commandos were flown undetected into Indian airspace. Each of the three groups consisted of approximately three officers, one junior commissioned officer[2] and 60 other ranks. At Pathankot, a border town near an important railhead in north Punjab, the commandos jumped at 0230 hours. Wind led to scattering, and the commandos could mount only a disorganized attack on the airbase. An officers' mess was blown apart, but the paratroopers failed to destroy any aircraft. Several of the commandos were captured, but most managed to exfiltrate back across the border.

At Adampur the paratroopers were detected immediately and could not launch their planned attack. Most men from this group were captured by the evening of 8 September. At Halwara, heavy winds carried the commandos nearly four miles from their target. Over the next two days nearly all of the paratroopers from this group were captured by Punjabi police. While the raids failed to destroy aircraft, they did cause confusion for the Indian defenders in Punjab.

(2) 'Junior Commissioned Officer' is a rank peculiar to the armies of South Asia. It was created during British colonial times as a link between the privileged officer class and the much less educated NCO cadre. India, Pakistan, and Bangladesh maintained this rank after independence.

India:
1: Skydiver, 10 Para Cdo.Bn., 1980s
2: Para Cdo. beret badge, 1960s
3: Pte., 1 Para Cdo. Bn., 1980s

1

2

3

A

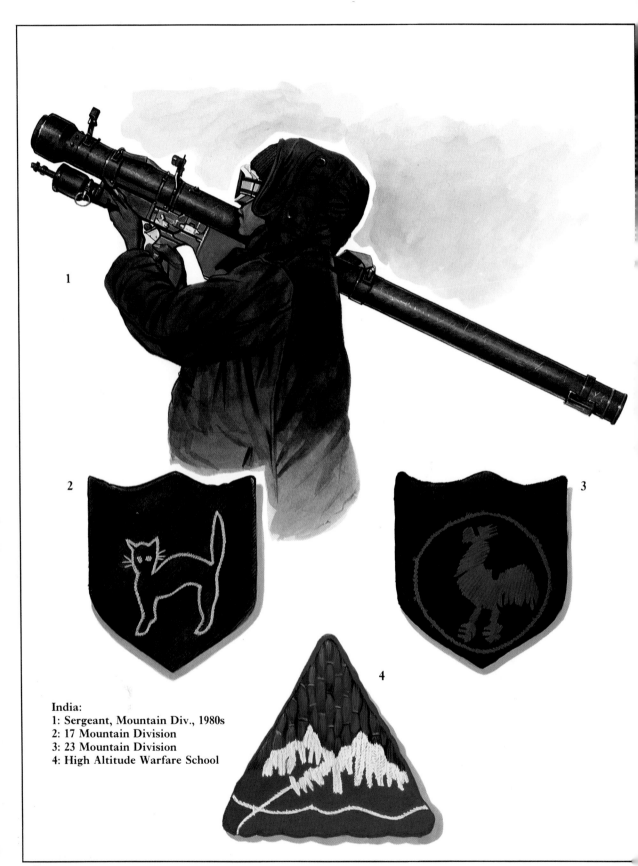

India:
1: Sergeant, Mountain Div., 1980s
2: 17 Mountain Division
3: 23 Mountain Division
4: High Altitude Warfare School

India:
1: Major, 54 Air Asslt. Div., 1987
2: 54 Air Assault Division
3: Paratrooper, Sri Lanka, 1989

C

India:
1: Brigadier, 50 Ind. Para Bde., 1988
2: Lt. Col., 6 Para Bn., 1989
3: Private, 6 Para Bn., 1988

1

2

3

D

India:
1: Inspector General, SFF, 1973
2: Commando, SFF, early 1970s
3: Special Frontier Force

E

India:
1: SAG commando, NSG, 1988
2: SAG sniper, NSG, 1988
3: National Security Guard

India:
1 & 2: IMSF commandos, 1988

G

Pakistan:
1: Commando, SSG, late 1980s
2: Commando, Musa Coy., late 1980s
3: Special Service Group beret badge

H

Pakistan:
1: Officer, SSG, 1990
2: Private, SSG, 1990
3: Brig. Tariq Mahmood, 1987

I

Pakistan:
1 & 2: Commandos, SSGN, late 1980s
3: Special Service Group (Navy)
   Training Centre

J

Sri Lanka:
1: Sgt., Commando Regt., 1989
2: Officer, Special Task Force, 1989
3: Private, STF, 1989

K

Afghanistan:
1: Sgt., Commando Bde., 1985
2: Commando insignia

1

2

3

4

Nepal:
3: Para Bn. beret badge, 1960s
4: Para Bn. hat badge, current

भैरवनाथ

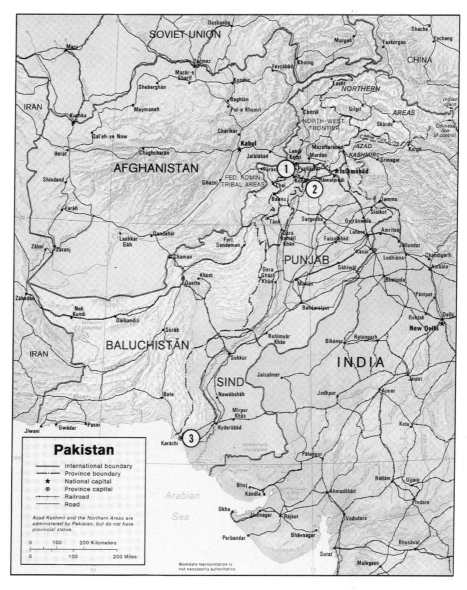

Map of Pakistan. The army airborne school is at Peshawar (1), the SSG headquarters at Cherat (2), and the SSGN headquarters at Karachi (3).

For the remainder of the war, 19 Baluch participated in small unit actions while attached to regular army formations.

The battalion, which had suffered relatively few casualties during the war, was expanded in 1966 and officially redesignated as the nucleus of a new, independent three-battalion Special Service Group. Each SSG battalion numbered 700 men and was commanded by a lieutenant-colonel; they were designated 1, 2, and 3 Commando Battalions. SSG Headquarters was maintained at Cherat.

1970–71

In December 1970 elections in East Pakistan gave a big majority to Bengali nationalists of the Awami League. After negotiations broke down over giving power to the elected officials, Bengalis began planning for civil unrest. Leading the unrest was the action arm of the Awami League, the Mukti Bahini ('Liberation Army'). Companies from the SSG rotated through East Pakistan dur-

ing the late 1960s on a regular basis. However, by 1970 the entire 2 Cdo. Bn. was sent to the East to counter the growing civil disturbances; they were replaced in January 1971 by 3 Cdo. Bn., which was posted to Comilla.

To re-establish government authority, the Pakistani Army in March 1971 increased its strength in the east to 60,000 men. On the night of 25/26 March Pakistani military units launched Operation 'Searchlight', designed to quell civil unrest and silence the Awami League. One company of 3 Cdo. Bn. was rushed to Dacca to begin the operation. At 0100 hours on 26 March a platoon from this company initiated the operation by raiding the house of Sheikh Mujibur Rahman, the leader of the Awami League. The commandos used rocket launchers to clear barriers blocking the road to the house, then neutralized the guards. Fifty commandos stormed inside and captured their target alive.

By the next day civil war in East Pakistan had begun in earnest. Bengali units of the military and police revolted, many of them joining the Mukti Bahini and attacking government posts. On 27

March a detachment from 3 Cdo. Bn. was sent to locate a column from 20 Baluch Bn. which was attacked while travelling from Comilla to Chittagong. The commandos were hit hard on infiltration, and were forced to abort the mission. Another commando detachment was sent to blow up the radio station at Chittagong, which was seized by Bengali nationalists. While attempting a waterborne approach into the city they were hit by rebel fire and suffered 16 dead.

During the final days of March the bulk of 3 Cdo. Bn. was brought from Comilla to Chittagong, where it joined the newly arrived 2 Cdo. Battalion. In often brutal urban warfare, the commandos and other Pakistani forces were generally able to re-assert authority in the cities, though at a huge cost in civilian lives. In the countryside, however, the Mukti Bahini, trained and supplied by India, had by August increased to a strength of nearly 100,000 guerrillas.

National Security Guard 'Black Cat' commandos firing on Punjabi terrorists, 1990. Weapons include the 7.62mm FN machine gun, the Heckler & Koch PSG-1 sniper rifle, and the Mk 4 Sterling. (Courtesy India Today)

During the summer 3 Cdo. Bn. was charged with clearing captured sections of the north-south highway leading to Chittagong. Attacking on foot or by helicopter, the entire battalion systematically began retaking the road. Towards the end of the operation, however, the commandos encountered heavy insurgent defences surrounding the Meghna River bridge. In addition, explosives had been planted along the bridge's columns. The commandos infiltrated the vicinity, stormed the rebel positions, and captured the bridge intact. To prove that the bridge was in friendly hands one of the battalion's company commanders, Maj. Tariq Mahmood (who would later become SSG Commander), stood atop a locomotive as it crossed the river.

By October the SSG began countering covert Indian support for the East Pakistani insurgents by conducting cross-border raids into Indian territory. Pakistani commandos reportedly derailed Indian trains near the border on 17 and 19 October. 3 Cdo. Bn. also launched successful heliborne raids against insurgent training camps in the vicinity of the Belonia Bulge during November. In late November the SSG was given contingency plans to destroy or damage the strategic Farakka Bridge in the event of an Indian incursion.

When the Indian invasion of East Pakistan materialized on 3/4

December, most of 3 Cdo. Bn. had already left East Pakistan, leaving 2 Cdo. Bn. at Kaptai to operate in the vicinity of the Chittagong Hill Tracts. There the battalion ran successful harassment missions from the hills. In addition, one commando platoon was attached to the headquarters of 39 Inf. Div. at Chandpur; this platoon attempted to exfiltrate by river to Dacca on 10 December, but was decimated by an Indian MiG-21 strike. When the Pakistanis surrendered in Dacca, some men from 2 Cdo. Bn. exfiltrated to Burma; others were taken prisoner and eventually repatriated.

In the western theatre, the Pakistani army launched an attack towards the Poonch sector from Kahuta; during this advance SSG detachments infiltrated behind Poonch to cut the road. The main Pakistani thrust, however, could not link up with the commandos, and the attack was called off. Smaller SSG teams were also active in the Sialkot sector, including a three-man deep penetration mission that located an Indian medium gun and directed effective counter-battery fire. This particular operation is mentioned in Indian Army commando courses as an example of a successful raiding operation. Further plans to use the SSG on deep penetration missions were aborted by the war's quick conclusion.

PAKISTANI SPECIAL FORCES SINCE 1971

Formation insignia posted outside 19 Baluch's headquarters, 1964; note that 'SSG' has been added below scroll, 'The Baluch Regiment'. (Courtesy Roger Seymour)

Following the 1971 War the SSG was next used during the 1973–1977 Baluchistan insurgency in western Pakistan. Supported by Afghanistan, the Baluchi insurgent movement reached a peak in late 1974. The government responded with massive counter-insurgency sweeps of the countryside, assisted by helicopters and crews sent by the Shah of Iran. Among the Pakistani units which saw heavy fighting were two SSG battalions kept on constant rotation. After a truce in November 1977 the insurgency subsided, and the SSG elements were withdrawn.

As worldwide terrorist incidents increased in the late 1970s an anti-terrorist role was added to the SSG mission. The assignment was given to the Musa Company, an independent formation within the SSG. The Musa Company, named after the prophet Moses, was originally formed in 1970 as a combat diver unit. In 1980, however, each SSG battalion raised a diver detachment and the Musa Company was converted into an anti-terrorist unit.

The Musa Company's baptism in its new role came on 30 September 1981 after Sikh terrorists hijacked an Indian Airlines jet to Lahore. Using a technique demonstrated by 4 Baluch Bn. during an earlier Pakistan hijacking, the commandos disguised themselves as a cleaning crew and boarded the plane. After a brief fight the five hijackers were arrested and all 44 hostages rescued in a flawless operation.

The Musa Company was next called into action in September 1986 when a New York-bound Pan Am 747 was hijacked by Palestinian terrorists in Karachi. The Musa commandos were sent to the airport and prepared for an assault on the aircraft. In addition, a US Army Delta team landed at Karachi on 5 September, but not before disaster struck. The plane's internal generator failed, plunging the aircraft into darkness. The panicked hijackers immediately began firing on the hostages and throwing grenades inside the cabin. Eighteen passengers were killed; the rest fled down escape chutes.

Because the Musa Company were rehearsing an aircraft assault on the opposite side of the airport, the passengers had already escaped before the SSG arrived at the plane. Unfortunately, some members of the SSG claimed early credit for 'raiding' the aircraft, a boast that was easily disproved.

Other units of the SSG have been used on various special missions during the 1980s. The SSG, for example, began in mid-1986 a large-scale basic training programme for Sri Lankan paramilitary militia forces. Commando and airborne training were given to members of the Sri Lankan Commando Regiment. In addition, SSG members have been seconded for covert operations in Afghanistan, as air marshals on Pakistan Airlines, and for VIP security. Some foreign observers noted that the effective strength of the SSG appeared to have suffered due to the large number of secondary assignments it received in the mid-1980s.

In 1986 the SSG was used to attack Indian positions on the contested Siachen Glacier. Again in September 1987, SSG elements were sent to storm the Indian trenches on the glacier. However, the Indians had intercepted Pakistani radio messages and located a team of mountaineers that was establishing three rope systems for the SSG. When the SSG arrived the alerted Indian garrison decimated the Pakistani commandos. Nineteen officers and men of the SSG were posthumously awarded gallantry medals for the action, including the Crescent of Valour, the second-highest operational award, given to an SSG captain.

Most recently, the SSG was used to quell street fighting in Karachi in April 1990. It is also suspected that SSG elements were brought to the frontline during the period of heightened tension along the Kashmir border in mid-1990.

At present, the SSG maintains its headquarters at Cherat and runs the Airborne School at Peshawar. Two SSG battalions are

Three US Army Special Forces advisors to 19 Baluch, 1964. After some of the Pakistani students allowed their hair to grow, these instructors donned black wigs in jest. (Courtesy Roger Seymour)

normally rotated through Cherat, with a third battalion divided between the border and other strategic locations such as the Tarbella Dam and nuclear research facilities. Each SSG battalion numbers 700 men, in four companies. Each company is split into platoons and further sub-divided into ten-man teams. Battalions are commanded by lieutenant-colonels; the Group currently is led by a colonel.

14 Para Bde. is attached to 8 Div. in Sialkot. It retains the airborne designation in name only; none of its battalions are paraqualified.

SSG Training

SSG officers must have at least two years of prior military experience and volunteer from other formations for three-year assignments with the SSG; NCOs and enlisted men volunteer from other formations to serve permanently in the SSG. All trainees must participate at an eight-month SSG course at Cherat.

The SSG course emphasizes tough physical conditioning. Included is a 36-mile march in 12 hours, a gruelling requirement that was first institutionalized by 19 Baluch. SSG students are also required to run five miles in 40 minutes with full gear. Following the SSG course, trainees must volunteer for Airborne School. The course lasts four weeks, with wings awarded after seven (five day, two night) jumps. Non-SSG airborne students only have to complete the five day jumps.

Many in the SSG are selected for additional specialist training. A HALO course is given at Peshawar, with a 'Skydiver' tab awarded after five freefall jumps. A 'Mountain Warfare' qualifi-

cation badge is given after completing a course at the Mountain Warfare School in Abbottad; and a 'Combat Diver' badge is awarded for a course held by the Naval Special Service Group (SSGN) at Karachi. Previously, when the Musa Company was a Combat Diver unit, it conducted its own scuba courses at Manora Navy Base in Karachi. At that time, three classes of combat swimmers were recognized: 1st class to those completing an 18-mile swim; 2nd class to those finishing a 12-mile swim; and 3rd class for a 6-mile swim.

After the Musa Company was converted to an anti-terrorist unit, it received training by British SAS advisors in Cherat during mid-1981. The SSG also regularly sends students to the US for special warfare and airborne training.

SSG Weapons and Uniform

Both 19 Baluch and the SSG have generally used the standard weaponry of the Pakistani army. By 1960, 19 Baluch was equipped with the US M-1 carbine. Once the SSG was created in 1966 a mix of British Sterling and Chinese-type AK-47s were in common use. Today, AK-47s and Pakistani-made copies of the German H&K series are most often seen.

While they were designated 19 Baluch the Pakistani special forces were distinguished by a green beret with the Baluch Regt. beret insignia on a maroon flash. A 'Baluch' tab, black with a maroon background, went on the left shoulder. Combat uniform was khaki. The SSG dropped the green Baluchi beret in favour of a maroon beret. A silver metal SSG beret badge is worn on a light blue felt square. A bullion SSG para wing with black cloth back-

Pakistan's SSG on parade, 1982. They are armed with the Chinese Type 56 assault rifle; note that the smocks are of the old 'Bhutto regime' camouflage pattern.

ground is worn on the left chest; a red cloth version is worn by master parachutists (50 jumps); SSG riggers wear an SSG wing with the English word 'Rigger' stitched across the wing. Non-SSG graduates from the Airborne School wear a wing based on the British Army design. Regulations forbid the wearing of any airborne-qualification wings from foreign armies. A distinctive SSG badge featuring a dagger framed by lightning bolts, used since at least 1964 by members of 19 Baluch, goes on the left shoulder; qualification tabs and badges (Skydiver, SCUBA, or Mountain Warfare) go on the right shoulder. A silver metal SSG insignia is occasionally worn on shoulder straps.

With the rise of the Bhutto regime in 1970, the SSG adopted a smock constructed from unique Pakistani camouflage material. This was worn until the mid-1980s; however, because the camouflage was associated with the previous regime, it was replaced in 1987 by a British DPM (Disruptive Pattern Material) camouflage smock. Khaki trousers were standard throughout the period. Musa Company anti-terrorist commandos wear a mix of black or grey combat uniforms.

In a country where the military has long played a dominant role in politics, the SSG is generally considered to be an apolitical unit. Some former members of the group have risen to prominence in the Army, and the former commander of the SSG, Brig. Tariq Mahmood, had close relations with the late Pakistan President Zia ul-Haq. Brigadier Mahmood, a popular, charismatic leader who commanded the SSG for a decade, had been twice awarded the Armed Forces' third-highest operational gallantry award for the 1965 and 1971 Wars, as well as the Armed Forces' fourth-highest non-operational award. He died in a demonstra-

tion freefall jump in May 1989 after his parachute failed to deploy properly.

Navy Special Forces

In 1966 the Pakistan Navy created its own commando unit, the Naval Special Service Group (SSGN). Training was initially conducted by the Army SSG at its Cherat, Peshawar, and Karachi bases. Because the Army SSG had its own scuba-qualified Musa Company at the time, the SSGN was given responsibility for the coast and the Musa Company was tasked with assignments along inland waterways in both East and West Pakistan. In the 1971 War the Musa Company was not used in combat; however, the SSGN saw action while attached to a short-lived Marine Battalion in Chittagong.

The SSGN currently maintains its headquarters in Karachi. Headed by a Pakistan Navy commander, it has a strength of one company and is assigned to unconventional warfare operations in the coastal regions. In war, the SSGN would make use of the Pakistan Navy's midget submarine fleet. SSGN parachute training is conducted by the Army SSG; all other training is held at the SSGN training centre, PNS *Iqbal*, in Karachi[3]. Some SSGN

(3) PNS denotes Pakistan Navy Ship; all Pakistan Navy training and support facilities are commissioned as ships.

SSG on parade, late 1980s. In 1987, SSG camouflage was changed to the British DPM pattern seen here. The four officers in the first row all wear the triangular mountain warfare patch on their right shoulder. Weapons are the Chinese Type 56-1 assault rifle.

Brig. Tariq Mahmood, SSG commander, 1988. He wears specialist qualification badges for skydiving and mountain warfare on his right shoulder, and the SSG parachute wing over his right pocket. Brigadier Mahmood was tragically killed in June 1989 when his parachute failed to deploy properly during a skydiving demonstration.

students are sent to the US for specialist courses. During the mid-1970s the SSGN held joint exercises with US Navy SEALS and the Imperial Iranian Navy.

The SSGN is distinguished by a dark blue beret with three versions of the 'fouled anchor' Navy beret badge for officers, NCOs, and enlisted men. A metal SSGN qualification badge featuring a vertical dagger superimposed over a midget submarine is worn over the left pocket on dress uniforms. Parachute wings are worn over the right pocket.

AFGHANISTAN

In early 1964 the Royal Afghan Armed Forces created its first élite formation, 242 Para Unit[1]; an independent army battalion, it was directly subordinate to the General Staff. Based at Sherpur Fort in the north-west outskirts of Kabul, the unit conducted airborne training in Kabul, Bagram, and Jalalabad. Command of the unit was given to Capt. Habib Bulah, who had just returned from the Infantry Officers' Advanced Course and airborne training at Fort Benning in the United States.

In the summer of 1967 the Afghan Army created a second élite formation, 444 Commando Unit. Because the Chief of Staff of 1 (Central) Corps had been instrumental in its creation this battalion-sized unit was kept under the direct control of the Central Corps; airborne-qualified, it was based at Bala Hissar Fort in the southern outskirts of Kabul. The commander was Lt.Col. Aqel Shah; he passed command during the following year to his chief of staff, Maj. Rahmatullah Safi[2].

(1) In public, Royal Afghan Army battalions were called 'sub-units'; regiments and independent reinforced battalions were called 'Units'; and independent brigades were called 'Forces'.
(2) Lt.Col. Aqel Shah assumed command of an independent Mountain Bde., which was also considered an élite formation.

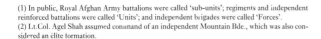

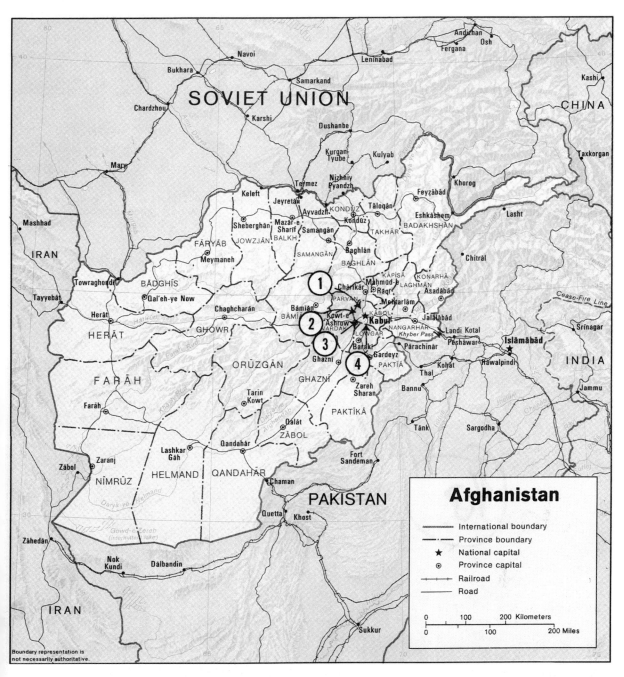

Map of Afghanistan. Sherpur Fort is north-west of Kabul (1); Mahtab Qala Garrison, west (2); Rishkoor Garrison, south-west (3); and the Bala Hissar Fort, south (4).

In 1972–73 a second commando formation, 455 Commando Unit, was being formed at the Bala Hissar; before it could come to full strength the coup d'état of July 1973 led to the overthrow of King Zahir and the installation of a Republican government under President Mohammad Daoud. During the coup, leftist junior officers within 242 Para Unit lent their support to the Republican forces; one of these airborne officers, Capt. Hashem Wardak, was promoted to major and given command of the battalion.

Within 444 Commando Unit, the Soviet-trained chief of operations, Capt. Faiz Mohammed, led part of the battalion in sup-port of Dauod during the coup. Promoted to the rank of major, he was given command of the unit and purged it of pro-Royalist elements. As a further reward Maj. Faiz soon became Minister of the Interior; command of the battalion was subsequently given to Maj. Hedayatullah. After being used briefly as a palace guard in Kabul, 444 Commando were relocated in 1974 to the city of Jala-

51

labad. Once they left Kabul, 455 Commando remained the only commando formation at the Bala Hissar, commanded by Maj. Hashem Zadran.

By 1975 two further commando units were established. 666 Commando Unit was based at Khandahar under the direct command of 2 Corps, and 777 Commando Unit was stationed at Paktia under 3 Corps. Both 444 Commando at Jalalabad and 455 Commando at the Bala Hissar remained under the control of Central Corps. In 1975 444 Commando saw its first combat while spearheading a counter-insurgency sweep against an uprising by fundamentalist Muslims in the Panjsher, a strategic valley north of Kabul.

In April 1978 President Daoud was killed in a coup d'état and replaced by a pro-Soviet communist government under Nur Mohammad Taraki. Communist sympathizers within 242 Para neutralized the battalion to ensure that it did not intervene on behalf of Dauod. Meanwhile, the Bala Hissar barracks were set on fire by pro-communists to distract and immobilize 455 Commando. Other commando battalions, because of their distance from Kabul, did not get involved in the coup.

In the immediate aftermath of the coup a reorganization and redesignation of élite units took place. 455 Commando and 242 Para were combined into the new 26 Para Regiment, stationed at the Bala Hissar. At the same time the three other commando units retained their numerical designations but were renamed commando regiments. Several of these élite units saw limited combat action against the growing anti-communist Mujahadeen rebel movement, including operations at around, Khost, and Nuristan.

By mid-1979 anti-communist dissent within the Afghan Army was beginning to grow. An uprising within the military was planned for the night of 5 August; however, the Kabul authorities uncovered the plot and quickly arrested several anti-communist officers. Word of the arrests did not reach the Bala Hissar and anti-communist elements in the garrison began the uprising on their own. Leading the rebellion were elements of 444 Cdo. Regt., part of which had been temporarily recalled to the Bala Hissar. The commandos clashed with pro-communists within 26 Para Regt. and 32 Motorized Rifle Regt., both stationed at the Bala

Current-style Afghan wings; bullion senior wings on a red background (top); basic silver metal wings (bottom).

Pakistan Army silver and pale blue airborne wings (top); SSG rigger wings, in silver with gold star and white and red lettering (bottom); and SSG formation insignia (right), in gold with silver blade—all insignia on black background.

Hissar. Kabul rushed in helicopter gunships, tanks, loyal AGSA intelligence units and paramilitary forces from the Ministry of the Interior. After a four-hour battle the revolt was crushed, leaving 400 dead.

Following the failed uprising, 444 Cdo. Regt. was redesignated 444 Cdo. Bn.; its commander was changed, and the battalion was moved from Kabul to the garrison at Sorobi, half way between Kabul and Jalalabad. The other two commando regiments were similarly redesignated commando battalions.

In September 1979 Taraki was ousted and replaced by Hafizullah Amin. Three months later Soviet armed forces invaded, killed Amin, and installed Babrak Karmal. The Soviet 105 Airborne Division, which secured Kabul, quickly neutralized Afghan Army units around the capital and met no initial resistance. On 1 January 1980, however, Soviet paratroopers confronted 26 Para Regt. at the Bala Hissar and ordered the Afghans to disarm; when the regiment refused, the Soviets moved in and annihilated the unit, reportedly capturing or killing 700 men.

In the immediate aftermath of the clash with the Soviets, 26 Para Regt. was officially disbanded and some of the surviving paratroopers were merged into a new élite unit, 37 Commando Brigade, under Col. Shahnawaz Tani. The airborne-qualified brigade, with an official strength set at three battalions, came under the direct command of the General Staff. With the Bala Hissar occupied by Soviet forces, the new commando brigade was stationed at Rishkoor Garrison, 15 miles south-west of Kabul.

During the same year, 81 Artillery Bde. was given airborne training and converted into 38 Cdo. Bde. under the command of Brig. Tawab Khan; the brigade was stationed at Mahtab Qala Garrison, near the Afghan Military High School on the western outskirts of Kabul. Elements of the brigade saw limited combat action across northern Afghanistan in 1980, but it was not until September 1982 that it saw heavy fighting against Mujahadeen rebels in the Panjsher.

By 1983 the commando brigades had proved themselves to be among the few reliable fighting units in the Afghan Army. As a result, they saw constant action—and suffered heavy casualties. During mid-August 37 Commando fought well around Paktia, then were heliborne into the city of Khost at the end of the month. The brigade again distinguished itself before being airlifted back to Kabul in October.

In 1984 the commandos again saw heavy action. In April a Soviet-Afghan task force, which included 37 Commando, launched Operation 'Panjsher 7'. The task force moved into the Panjsher along several fronts, clearing parts of the valley for the first time since 1979. During late August 38 Commando were called upon to break the siege at Ali Khel in Paktia province. In December an unidentified commando battalion—possibly 444 Cdo. Bn., still stationed at Sorobi—was on operations in the Kunar valley.

By 1985 a Soviet shift toward small-unit tactics led to a further increase in Afghan commando operations. However, heavy casualties were beginning to take a toll. That spring 444 Cdo. Bn. reportedly suffered 80 per cent casualties during fighting in the Panjsher. Meanwhile, a Soviet/Afghan task force moved into the Kunar Valley during May in an attempt to break the siege at Barikot and seal part of the Afghan-Pakistan border. Although the Barikot siege was broken in June, 73 heliborne Afghan commandos were killed and 30 captured.

The Afghan commandos continued to be heavily committed for the remainder of the year. In June 38 Cdo. Bde. was forced to retreat while performing garrison duties at Pechgur in the

Officer from an Afghan commando brigade, 1989. He wears a standard Afghan Army grey wool uniform and cap badge. Note the gold metal senior parachute wings on red felt background over his right pocket (Courtesy India Today). See also Osprey Men-at-Arms 178, Russia's War in Afghanistan, for photo and colour plates of camouflage uniforms.

Panjsher. Meanwhile, 37 Cdo. Bde. was sent to reinforce Khost in July. During the following month 37 Bde., together with 466 Cdo. Bn. (formerly called 666 Cdo. Bn.) flown in from Khandahar, participated in the year's second major eastern offensive.

In March 1986 Soviet paratroopers joined forces with 37 Cdo. Bde. and 466 Cdo. Bn. from Khandahar in a major operation to capture the Mujahadeen guerrilla base at Zhawar on the Afghan-Pakistan border. 37 Commando, which spearheaded the initial attacks in April, had one of its three battalions decimated when it was heliborne directly onto a guerrilla stronghold. The remainder of the brigade successfully led the final push to capture Zhawar. By the end of 1986 further Afghan commando detachments had been raised and attached as reconnaissance units to larger Afghan and Soviet infantry formations.

In late 1988, in anticipation of the Soviet withdrawal from Afghanistan, the Kabul government formed a new Special Guard as a last line of defence around the capital. Set at a strength of six brigades, the Special Guard was composed of loyalists to Afghan strongman Najibullah; units reportedly incorporated into the Special Guard include the Presidential Guard Brigade, militarized members of the communist party, and personnel from the commando brigades. Despite media reports to the contrary, both commando brigades have retained their independent status and were not incorporated into the Special Guard. The commando brigades were moved to the Bala Hissar following the departure of Soviet forces in February 1989.

As Kabul's mobile reserve, the Special Guard were used in many of the major battles against the Mujahadeen during 1989, including the sieges of Jalalabad and the Salang Pass. Increasingly, however, the Najibullah regime relied less on the army and instead made use of more loyal units from the national guard, military units of State Security, and 53 Div. (a militia unit composed along ethnic lines). In 1989 the army raised a new forma-

tion, 61 Strike Regt.; like the commando brigades, this saw only limited offensive action.

During March 1990 Defence Minister Shahnawaz Tani led a failed coup attempt in Kabul. As he was the original commander of 37 Cdo. Bde., Tani was quick to gain the support of his old unit. In the aftermath of the uprising the brigade commander was arrested, though the brigade itself was apparently not disbanded. 61 Strike Regt. had also sided with Tani, and its commander was arrested.

Training for the commandos is currently conducted around Kabul, including airborne jumps conducted in Kabul and Bagram. In early 1989 there were unconfirmed reports of a Vietnamese military delegation training Afghan 'commandos'.

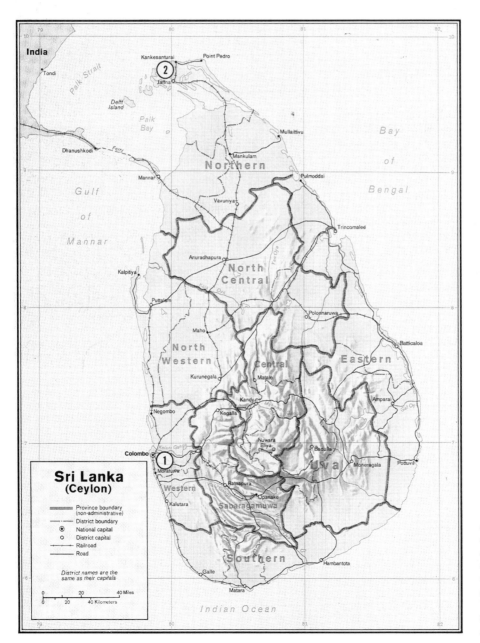

Map of Sri Lanka. Sri Lankan Commando Regiment headquarters is located at Ganemulla, outside Colombo (1). The heaviest fighting against Tamil Tiger guerrillas has taken place on the Jaffna Peninsula (2).

SRI LANKA

Army Commando Regiment

In 1977 the Sri Lankan government began forming its own airlines, Airlanka. Because of the threat of international hijackings the government also wanted to create a hostage-rescue team. An advance British Mobile Training Team was despatched to Colombo in 1978 and determined that such a unit should be created within the army. By year's end, an embryonic hostage-rescue squadron had been formed with three officers and three other men. A second class was trained, adding three more officers and 15 men. Most of these personnel were sent in 1979 to Agra, India, for parachute training. In 1980 12 British Special Air Service personnel arrived in Sri Lanka to provide four months of counter-terrorist training to the new squadron. Forty men were trained, plus a 40-man reserve.

Until 1983 the squadron focused on its hostage-rescue role. After 13 soldiers were killed by Tamil terrorists in July 1983, however, the commandos were also used as a counter-insurgency force in the north.

By 1985 the squadron had expanded to 100 men. On 16 March 1986 the squadron was again expanded into the Commando Regiment. It was not until May 1987 that the regiment underwent its baptism of fire, which took place during Operation 'Liberation', the Sri Lankan army's major sweep against Tamil Tiger guerrilla strongpoints on the Jaffna Peninsula. While the main seaborne infantry thrust came from the west, 180 commandos were infiltrated in rubber boats on the north-east coast to act as a blocking force. The operation met with much success, but a diplomatic agreement with India in July 1987 forced the Sri Lankan army to move out of Tamil-dominated areas in the north.

For the next three years the commandos saw only limited action against the 'People's Liberation Front', a Sinhalese Marxist terrorist group operating in the deep south. In addition, 20 commandos were used for perimeter defence around the naval base at Trincomalee on the east coast.

Commanded by a lieutenant-colonel, the regiment falls far short of its authorized strength of 1,000 men. The core of the regiment is its four authorized assault groups; because of personnel shortages, however, the regiment could raise only three groups, lettered A through C. Each group, numbering 45–50 commandos, is led by a major or a captain. In June 1988, again because of personnel shortages, the three groups were further consolidated into two groups: the regiment has plans to reform a third group in the future. Currently, one group remains in Ganemulla on alert for hostage-rescue operations; the other group is available for other missions within the country. For normal operations, each group is broken into detachments of four officers and ten men. In addition to the assault groups the regiment has two support groups: the Operations and Intelligence Group, commanded by a major, has three officers and 30 men; the Commando Regiment Training School, also commanded by a major, has six officers and 49 men.

Despite the pressure to expand quickly, commando training remains intensive. Selection begins with volunteers from the army taking an aptitude test; of these, 60 per cent pass. A 34-day selection course follows, with a drop-out rate of 75 per cent. Those who have survived then face 18–20 weeks of training at the Commando Regiment's 45-acre headquarters at Ganemulla, near Colombo's international airport. Hostage-rescue training lasts an

Monument to Sri Lankan army commandos killed in action, located at the Cdo. Regt. headquarters, Ganemulla. The statue was adopted from a British SAS statue, with an actual Chinese Type 56-1 assault rifle added.

additional 16 weeks. In 1986, because of the need to expand the armed forces quickly, the commandos were forced to alter their recruitment policy by taking volunteers straight after high school.

The Sri Lankan commandos have sent several personnel overseas for training. In 1985 four members went to the US for Special Forces training, while three went to Ranger training. In addition, Keeny Meeny Services, a British security firm partly staffed by former SAS soldiers, gave counter-insurgency training in 1985 to the regiment's B Group. During the following year two officers and 28 men went to Pakistan for six months of SSG training. Another officer has been sent to England for training with the Royal Marines.

By 1987 few in the regiment were airborne-qualified; during

Members of the Sri Lankan Cdo. Regt. dressed for a counter-terrorist mission, 1989; they are armed with the Heckler & Koch MP-5. Barely visible is the yellow 'Commando' tab, in Sinhalese script, on the right shoulder of the closest commando.

that year, however, the regiment began to stockpile T-10 parachutes, and at the same time two riggers and two jumpmasters were qualified in Pakistan. In July 1988 an Indian jumpmaster was dispatched to Colombo to oversee parachute training; something less than half of the regiment is now airborne-qualified. Training jumps are normally conducted from Chinese-made Y-12 transports; five day jumps must be made to earn parachute wings.

The commandos are well equipped. Since 1980 Sri Lankan commandos have used Heckler and Koch MP-5 sub-machine-guns, sometimes fitted with silencers. Snipers are provided with the Heckler & Koch 63 or Steyr automatic rifle.

Commandos wear a variety of olive drab and camouflage uniforms, including British and Pakistani patterns. A maroon beret is worn with a badge bearing the motto 'Nothing is impossible'. Parachute wings are worn on working dress uniforms; a new wing

design was introduced when the squadron was expanded to a regiment in March 1986.

In 1985 the Sri Lankan army explored the idea of creating another élite commando unit to specialize in deep-penetration reconnaissance. For the next five years, however, the Commando Regt. continued to fulfil this mission. In 1990, 600 men were reportedly assigned as the nucleus of a new Special Forces Regt. to handle reconnaissance missions; however, with the Sri Lankan army short of funding and personnel, this new regiment was still unformed as of 1992.

Also in 1985, the Sri Lankan Air Force attempted to form a 30-man heliborne commando unit. Not coincidentally, the commander of this unit was the brother of the commander of the army's Commando Regiment. During that same year, however, the commander was killed in a helicopter rappelling accident; the concept of an air force commando unit died along with him.

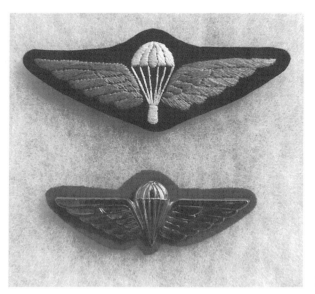

Sri Lankan parachute wings: Commando Squadron wing (top) in white and blue on black; yellow metal Commando Regiment wing on red felt backing (bottom), issued in 1986. The regimental wing comes only in the metal version and is made in Pakistan.

Special Task Force

In August 1980 two special platoons were organized in the Sri Lankan police. These platoons were grouped into a 100-man commando force in 1983. Considered an élite outfit, the force was organized in part to counter-balance the army after rumours of a military coup d'état were heard in the capital. Significantly, the President's son was a chief advisor to the police commandos.

In February 1983 the Special Task Force (STF) was established as a separate division within the police. When Tamil Tiger guerrillas killed 13 soldiers in Jaffna in July the STF was sent to the north. During the following year the STF underwent counter-insurgency training by Keeny-Meeny Services. After training the STF moved to the Eastern Province, where they remained in strength until July 1987. During this period the 4,000-man STF gained a reputation as a brutal yet effective counter-guerrilla organization. In 1988 STF detachments were located both in the east, and in the deep south against Marxist insurgents. Following the departure of the IPKF in 1990 the STF was sent back to the north, seeing heavy action against Tamil guerrillas. The STF also provided VIP security in Colombo during the late 1980s.

The STF is currently larger than regimental strength. It is most often used in companies, platoons, or sections. The STF accepts volunteers from the Police Academy; its own training camp lasts an additional 12–18 weeks. Keeny-Meeny Services advisors remained attached to the STF training camp until 1987.

Because of the force's privileged political status STF commandos are well equipped. The standard weapons are the M-16 and the Heckler & Koch 63 sub-machinegun. STF units also use 60mm mortars. Reflecting the British influence, the STF normally wears British DPM camouflage; headgear is a green beret, earning the STF the nickname 'Green Tigers'. The beret insignia carries the motto 'Overcome'.

NEPAL

As part of a modernization programme within the Royal Nepalese Army (RNA), the first group of 15 officers and NCOs were sent to Israel for airborne training on 21 August 1965; in February 1966 a second group of 100 trainees followed them. On the following day a Parachute Company and a Para Training School were established in the RNA. During 1968–69 the paratroopers were expanded into a battalion, along with a Headquarters and Training School. All were located in Katmandu. While they have not participated in any combat, the paras dropped men and supplies during natural disasters, and disarmed Tibetan resistance fighters operating on Nepalese soil during the early 1970s. In addition, the training centre gave basic instruction to the Nepalese king in 1969.

On 11 March 1975 the Parachute Bn. received the colours of the Bhairab Nath ('Sky God') Regt., which had been established in 1849. Since then, the unit has officially been known as the Bhairab Nath Battalion (Airborne). Until 1981 it came directly under Army Headquarters; in 1982, however, the battalion was merged into the RNA Support Brigade in Katmandu. In 1985 the battalion was placed in the 1st Brigade at Katmandu.

The battalion currently consists of four rifle companies, lettered A to D. In addition there is a headquarters company, which includes a mortar platoon, machine gun platoon, anti-tank platoon, quartermaster platoon, and transportation platoon. Command of the battalion is held by a lieutenant-colonel, as is that of the Training School. Parachute training lasts six weeks, including eight day jumps and two night jumps.

BANGLADESH

The Bangladesh Armed Forces (BAF) traces its origins to early 1971 when most of the Bengalis serving in the East Bengal Regiment, the East Pakistan Rifles, and the East Pakistan Police revolted against the government rule. Many joined the Mukti Bahini, the nationalist guerrilla movement supported by India.

Following the 1971 Indo-Pakistan War the BAF absorbed dozens of Bengali members of the Pakistani Special Service Group, as well as combat swimmer-qualified personnel. Because of limited funding and shortages in transport aircraft, Dhaka[1] refrained from forming an airborne unit. A limited number of combat swimmers were retained; their qualification insignia was unchanged from the triangular Pakistani SSG combat swimmer badge.

During the early 1980s the BAF fielded five infantry divisions; of these, 24 Inf. Div. in Chittagong was engaged in counter-insurgency operations in the Chittagong Hill Tracts. To pacify the Chittagong region, the BAF by 1983 was training an average of 50 infantry officers and other ranks annually in counter-insurgency, jungle warfare and commando tactics at its Special Warfare Wing.

In the summer of 1986 the military-led Bangladeshi government formed an élite task force for VIP protection. Composed of

(1) The capital city of Dacca changed its spelling to Dhaka after independence.

Sri Lankan Cdo. Regt. insignia: beret badge (top) and 'collar dogs' have silver bayonets, gold wreath and black backing.

The essentially similar but unwreathed qualification chest badge (centre) is on red backing.

THE PLATES

India:

A1: Skydiver, 10 Para Commando Battalion, 1980s
Outfitted for a High Altitude, Low Opening parachute jump, this para commando wears a black jumpsuit, helmet, wrist altimeter, and square-canopy parachute with US leaf pattern camouflage cover, all of which were purchased commercially from Western nations. His weapon is the 7.62mm SLR, some of which were imported from England and some of which were made in India from the Belgian FN FAL design. The 'Commando' tab on his shoulder indicates that he belongs to one of the three para commando battalions; the Western Command insignia below the tab confirms that he is a member of 10 Para Commando Battalion.

A2: Beret badge, Para Commandos, 1960s
From the mid-1960s to the mid-1970s 9 and 10 Para Cdo. Bns. wore a unique badge on a maroon beret. The design was an exact copy of the British SAS badge, with the motto 'Sacrifice' written in Hindi. By the late 1970s this badge had been phased out; instead, the para commandos are now issued the standard beret badge of the Parachute Regiment.

A3: Private, 1 Para Commando Battalion, 1980s
Because the para commando battalions are raised by the Parachute Regiment, it is often hard to distinguish a para commando from a normal paratrooper. Both wear maroon berets with the Parachute Regiment cap badge, and parachute wings over the right chest pocket. Those who go through the specialized army commando course—a requirement for the para commandos, an option for paratroopers—wear the commando qualification badge on the right pocket (see Plate D2). Only active members of para commando battalions, however, wear 'Commando' tabs on the shoulders. In the field para commandos, as here, often wear black uniforms with black head bandanas. His weapon is the Indian 7.62mm SLR with a US-made night scope.

B1: Sergeant, Mountain Division, 1980s
Stationed across the world's tallest mountain range, the Indian Army's mountain troops must dress for the frigid weather. In addition, because of the thin air, they cannot carry heavy loads. This private wears the standard issue winter parka with snow goggles. He holds a Soviet SA-7 anti-aircraft missile. No formation or qualification insignia are worn on winter uniforms. At lower elevations, mountain troops wear the beret and cap badge of their parent regiment (infantry regiments normally wear olive drab or dark green berets; paratroopers wear maroon berets). Mountain Division formation insignia appear on the left shoulder; the patch for the High Altitude Warfare School is sometimes worn on the right shoulder.

B2: Formation insignia, 17 Mountain Division

B3: Formation insignia, 23 Mountain Division

B4: High Altitude Warfare School

C1: Major, 54 Air Assault Division, 1987
Taken from a photo of the initial deployment of 54 Air Assault Div. to Sri Lanka in August 1987, this major wears the normal

82 officers and led by a Brigadier, the unit reportedly held wide powers, including arrest without warrant. Immediately criticized by the political opposition as an instrument of intimidation, nothing further has been heard of the unit.

By the late 1980s the BAF was eager to form a small heliborne commando unit, citing Bangladesh's need for an airmobile formation given the numerous rivers and frequent floods which hinder ground transportation. Budgetary restraints apparently delayed formation of the unit; in 1987, however, a dozen BAF students completed commando and parachute training at Indonesia's Batu Djardjar Special Forces Training Centre. In 1989, 30 more students were sent to Batu Djardjar for Jump Master training. During the same year Dhaka quietly began approaching foreign nations for assistance in forming an airborne unit; to date, however, such a unit is still waiting to be formed.

Suggested Reading

Defenders of Pakistan (Serozsons, 1988).
The Indian Army (Lancer, 1990).
K. C. Praval *Indian Army After Independence* (Lancer, 1987).
K. C. Praval *India's Paratroopers* (Thomson, 1974).
Rajesh Kadian *India's Sri Lanka Fiasco* (Vision, 1990).
S. S. Uban *Phantoms of Chittagong* (Allied, 1985).
Lachman Singh *Victory in Bangladesh* (Natraj, 1981).
Mark Urban *War in Afghanistan* (St. Martin's, 1988).
Siddiq Salik *Witness to Surrender* (Oxford, 1977).

Indian Army green uniform with the divisional insignia on the left shoulder and a plastic nameplate over the right pocket. His cap badge is that of 11 Gorkha Regiment, indicating that the major is probably a company commander from a battalion of 11 Gorkha Regt. assigned to 54 Air Assault Division.

C2: Formation insignia, 54 Air Assault Division

C3: Paratrooper, Sri Lanka, 1989

Taken from a photo of an Indian paratrooper during a major sweep of Sri Lanka's eastern coast in July 1989, he wears Indian Army khakis and a maroon beret with Parachute Regt. cap badge. The AK-47 suggests that he belongs to a para commando battalion. In addition, the snaps on the shoulders are probably for 'Commando' tabs which have been removed while on combat operations.

D1: Brigadier F. F. C. Bulsara, 50 Independent Para Brigade, 1988

During the Maldives operation Brig. Bulsara accompanied 6 Para Bn. on its flight from Agra to Hulule Airport. It is interesting to note that, aside from the parachute wings and commando qualification badge on his right pocket, he wears no other insignia, including the formation insignia of his para brigade. Note also that he has procured a unique camouflage uniform, not seen among any other members of the Parachute regiment.

D2: Lieutenant-Colonel, 6 Para Battalion, 1989

Taken from a photo of the commemoration ceremony for 6 Para Bn. after its one-year tour in the Maldives, the battalion commander is seen wearing Indian DPM camouflage and dress shoes. Note the parachute wings over the right pocket, and the commando qualification badge on the right pocket. The latter features a flaming dagger with the motto 'Sacrifice' written in Hindi. No formation insignia is worn on the right shoulder, indicating that 6 Para Bn. was not at that time subordinate to a brigade or division. For unknown reasons the commander is not wearing the Parachute Regt. badge on his beret.

D3: Private, 6 Para Battalion, 1988

Photographed on the first day of the Maldives operation, this private holds the Indian-made version of the 7.62mm FN FAL rifle. Extra magazines are carried in green Indian-made canvas pouches. The Indian DPM camouflage is now available to all military units stationed in tropical and temperate regions of the

Nepalese paratroopers in training; like the Indian army, they are armed with the 7.62mm FN FAL. Nepalese camouflage was originally purchased from Japan; the uniforms are now made in Nepal, but retain the same camouflage pattern as worn by the Japanese Self-Defense Forces.

country; a brown and tan variation has been issued to some units in the western desert region.

E1: Inspector General, SFF, 1973
Command of the SFF is held by an Indian Army general holding the title of 'SFF Inspector General'; the same general held this position for the SFF's first ten years. Pictured here in 1973, he wears Indian Army dress greens; the dark blue/red turban and gold cap badge are standard for general grade Sikh officers. He wears major-general's rank insignia on the shoulders. Curiously, he has placed the unique SFF 'Winged dagger' on his left shoulder; at the time, it was standard Indian practice to wear wings on the right shoulder.

E2: Commando, SFF, early 1970s
This Tibetan commando wears standard Indian Army fatigues with a black helmet used during parachute jumps, his name stencilled on the helmet. The weapon is the Sterling Mk 4, which at that time had started to replace the US M-1 within the SFF. The initials 'SFF' are displayed on both shoulders; in addition, the SFF formation insignia is worn on the left shoulder, and the unique SFF parachute wing on the right shoulder.

E3: Formation sign, SFF
Issued since the formation of the SFF in 1962, the SFF formation sign features the mythical Tibetan snow lion and flaming Tibetan sword.

F1: SAG Commando, NSG, 1988
Taken from a photo of an NSG counter-terrorist commando, he wears a black zippered jacket with a British armour vest. A radio is carried in his right sleeve pocket. The weapon is the Heckler & Koch MP-5 A2, with an additional clip attached 'duplex-style'. No insignia are worn on the combat uniform.

F2: SAG Sniper, NSG, 1988
Photographed during the 1988 Golden Temple operation, this SAF sniper holds a Heckler & Koch 7.62mm PSG-1 sniper rifle with telescopic sights. Snipers were used to pin down the Sikh extremists inside the temple during the first three days of the operation. All the NSG commandos at the Golden Temple wore black fatigues without insignia, British armour vests, and black helmets.

F3: Formation sign, NSG
First seen in 1990, the 'Black Cat' patch is worn by the NSG Special Ranger Group on the left shoulder.

G1: Commando, IMSF, 1988
Taken from a photo of IMSF commandos at their Bombay training camp in September 1988, this commando is armed with a US-made commercial crossbow with scope. Contrary to standard Indian practice the IMSF formation insignia is worn on the right, rather than left, shoulder. On dress uniforms IMSF personnel wear the gold metal combat diver badge over the left pocket and gold and silver bullion parachute wings over the right pocket.

G2: Commando, IMSF, 1988
Photographed after arresting fleeing Sri Lankan mercenaries on a hijacked boat during the Maldives operation, this IMSF com-

Sri Lankan commando officers inspect Chinese Type 56-1 assault rifles, 1989. The officer in front wears British DPM camouflage, the rest olive drab fatigues. Most of the men wear maroon berets and right shoulder lanyards and have commando qualification badges over their right pocket. Non-commando personnel performing administrative tasks for the Cdo. Regt. (such as the trooper second from the left in the rear row) wear black berets and have no qualification badge or lanyard.

mando is dressed no differently from a regular Indian infantryman. The weapon is an Indian-made Sterling Mk 4 with extra magazines in Indian canvas pouches. He wears Indian DPM camouflage, although most in the IMSF (including several others seen in the Maldives operation) prefer plain black fatigues. As a Sikh he wears an olive drab turban on operations; non-Sikh members of the IMSF normally wear a black/dark blue beret with the standard Indian Navy cap badge.

Pakistan:
H1: Commando, SSG, late 1980s
This commando wears the British DPM camouflage smock standardized during the Zia regime. He wears the SSG beret badge on a light blue flash—all companies within the SSG use the same flash; metal SSG titles appear on the shoulders; the unique SSG wing is worn over the right pocket. Additional qualification badges, such as combat swimmer, skydiver, and mountain warfare, go on the right shoulder. Not visible is the SSG formation sign on the left shoulder. The weapon is the Chinese Type 56-1 assault rifle.

H2: Commando, Musa Company, late 1980s
Since its conversion from a combat swimmer unit the Musa Company has been the SSG's counter-terrorist formation. This commando wears a British DPM shirt, Western body armour and a gasmask, and carries an H&K MP-5 A3 sub-machinegun. The metal shoulder titles are the only SSG insignia worn.

H3: Beret badge, SSG

I1: Officer, SSG, 1990
Taken from a photo of SSG personnel deployed to Karachi in the spring of 1990 to control rioting, this officer is wearing US camouflage, a pattern not often seen in the SSG. He has embellished his uniform by adding the tab 'PAK ARMY' above his left pocket. The SSG formation insignia is on his left shoulder; SSG rigger wings are above the right pocket. The SSG beret badge is worn on a light blue felt square.

I2: Private, SSG, 1990
Taken from the same photo during the Karachi rioting, this SSG private wears standard Pakistan Army tan fatigues. His weapon is the Chinese Type 56-1 assault rifle. Note the Chinese-made AK-47 magazine chest pouch, and the Mountain Warfare qualification badge on his right shoulder and the SSG formation sign on his left shoulder.

I3: Brigadier Tariq Mahmood, 1987
Brig. Mahmood, commander of the SSG, is shown addressing the Pakistani Command and Staff College in March 1987. On his right shoulder are the Skydiver and Mountain Warfare qualification insignia; over his right pocket are SSG wings. Though not seen here, those wounded in battle wear a red or yellow ribbon (depending on severity) below the wing.

J1: Commando, SSGN, late 1980s
This commando wears the standard SSGN light blue/white fatigues. On the left shoulder is the fouled anchor of the Pakistan Navy; on the right, the qualification insignia for clearance diving. On the dark blue/purple SSGN beret is worn a red Pakistan Navy fouled anchor cap badge, indicating a non-commissioned officer. The weapon is the Heckler & Koch G3 rifle. On dress uniforms the SSGN wears airborne wings, and the SSGN qualification badge featuring a miniature submarine superimposed on an upright dagger.

J2: Commando, SSGN, late 1980s
Taken from a photo of a seaborne infiltration exercise, this SSGN non-commissioned officer carries a Heckler & Koch 7.62mm G3 rifle with the barrel taped to keep out water. His field pack is standard Pakistan Army issue. Note life vest around his neck.

J3: Insignia, SSGN Training Centre

Sri Lanka:
K1: Sergeant, Commando Regiment, 1989
By the late 1980s a wide variety of uniforms could be seen in the Commando Regt., including olive drab fatigues as well as Pakistani, British, and South Korean camouflage. The local Sri Lankan batik industry even experimented in producing a vivid camouflage pattern in green, black, and purple for the commandos. This sergeant wears standard army olive drab fatigues with

Nepalese para formation insignia: original para battalion insignia (left) in black on scarlet; later issue battalion insignia (right)—green canopy, white lines, pale blue wings, black kukris, on maroon. Both are now obsolete; the para battalion wears the 1 Brigade shoulder insignia featuring a bow and arrow on a green square.

Sri Lankan-made boots; South Korean-made boots are also worn. Over his right pocket is the commando qualification badge; above this are jump wings. On his maroon beret is the Commando Regt. cap badge. Tabs on both shoulders have the word 'Commando' in yellow lettering; Commando Regt. badges are worn on both collars. His weapon is the Chinese Type 56-1.

K2: Officer, Special Task Force, 1989
The STF working uniform is dark brown with a green belt and round silver buckle. A tab reading 'Special Task Force' goes over the right pocket; the tab was made in England as part of the STF's contract with the British firm Keeny-Meeny Service. (The STF's British connection, in fact, resulted in over 30 items—ranging from camouflage cloth to insignia to duffel bags, and tea cups with the STF logo—being imported from England, at prices far higher than similar items made in Sri Lanka!) In the field, STF commandos normally wear camouflage uniforms made from British DPM cloth. The officer shown here wears the STF green beret with cloth police badge; a silver metal version also exists. Police rank insignia are worn on the shoulders.

K3: Private, Special Task Force, 1989
Whereas the Sri Lankan army is largely equipped with Chinese small arms, the STF is outfitted with more modern Western equipment. This trooper carries a South African Armscor 40mm six-shot grenade launcher. Slung is an M-16; the STF also use the CAR-15, and the Singaporean SAR 80 assault rifle. His camouflage uniform and matching cap are made from British DPM cloth. As is common among STF commandos in the field, his uniform is devoid of all insignia.

Afghanistan:
L1: Sergeant, Commando Brigade, 1985
In 1964 242 Para Unit was issued locally-made one-piece olive drab coveralls inspired by the Soviet airborne type. Metal airborne wings on a black cloth backing were worn over the right chest. When 444 Commando Unit was created in 1967 it initially wore the standard Afghan army khaki uniform. Metal airborne wings on a light blue cloth backing were worn over the right chest. A distinctive commando formation insignia (see Plate L2) appeared on the right shoulder.

In 1969 the commandos became the first Afghan army unit to adopt a spotted 'duck hunter' camouflage two-piece uniform; initially imported from the USSR, these were later manufactured locally. Within a year the paratroopers also started wearing the same camouflage. By mid-1970 a second camouflage pattern was issued to the commandos, this one a unique orange-green 'splinter' pattern manufactured in Afghanistan.

Following the 1979 Soviet invasion all attempts at dress standardization ceased as the Afghan commandos were issued a motley assortment of uniforms including limited supplies of the earlier two camouflage patterns, standard Afghan army wool uniforms, and the new-issue Soviet camouflage tunic and trousers. In addition, beginning in 1985, Bulgarian camouflage (tailored to Afghan army specifications) was issued to elements of both commando brigades.

At present Afghan commandos still wear airborne wings over the right breast. Several versions of the wings have been seen, including simple metal, sewn bullion, and metal wings with red, black, or light blue cloth backings: there no longer appears to be any significance to the colour of the cloth backing, although red is that most often seen in the commando brigades. Commandos are issued a maroon beret, pulled down to the right and worn with a large metal Afghan army badge. The commando formation insignia is worn on the right shoulder.

L2: Afghan Commando insignia
First worn by 444 Commando Unit in 1967, this insignia is now used by all commando formations. The script is the English word 'commando' phonetically transcribed into Pushtun.

Nepal:
L3: Para Battalion beret badge
On tactical exercises the RNA Para Battalion wear locally-manufactured camouflage uniforms with jungle hats; the camouflage is a direct copy of that used by the Japan Self-Defense Forces. On parachute jumps Israeli steel helmets are worn. The working dress uniform for the paratroopers consists of standard RNA olive drab fatigues. Until 1970 an Israeli-style red beret was worn. Since then, the battalion has switched to a Gurkha hat with one side of the brim fastened up. Until the early 1980s the Para

Battalion cap badge featured the Hindu sky god Bhairab Nath, seen here; the words 'Bhairab Nath' are printed on the bottom. This was originally worn without a flash on the beret, and with a square red flash on the Gurkha hat. In 1982, after the Para Battalion was subordinated to the Support Brigade, the battalion's original formation sign featuring a dragon and a parachute was briefly used as a cap badge.

L4: Nepalese Para Battalion hat badge
Currently, the parachute battalion uses this sewn badge on its Gurkha hats. The design was adopted from a now obsolete shoulder insignia for the battalion.

Bangladeshi insignia: parachute wing, silver and gold on black, worn in 1989 (top); combat swimmer qualification badge (bottom)—gold on dark blue, tank outlines and harpoon head red, black and white details. The combat swimmer badge is a nearly identical copy of the Pakistani SSG combat swimmer qualification badge.

Notes sur les planches en couleur

A1 Combinaison de saut noire, casque, altimètre de poignet et parachute à calotte carrée avec bâche de camouflage au motif feuillu US. Pour arme le SLR de 7,62 mm, l'écusson de "Commando" et l'insigne de Commandant Occidental indiquent qu'il fait partie du 10e Bataillon de Commando Parachutiste. **A2** Une réplique exacte de l'écusson britannique SAS, avec la devise "Sacrifice" écrite en hindi. **A3** Uniforme noir avec foulard noir de coiffure et un SLR indien de 7,62 mm avec portée de nuit de fabrication américaine.

B1 Parka d'hiver de distribution standard avec lunettes d'alpiniste. Pour arme le missile soviétique anti-aérien SA-7, l'insigne de formation de la Division Alpine apparaît sur l'épaule gauche.

C1 Uniforme vert courant de l'Armée indienne avec insigne de division sur l'épaule gauche et plaque d'identité en plastique sur la poche droite. L'écusson du képi est celui de la SFF sur l'épaule gauche. **C2** Combinaison kaki de l'Armée indienne et béret rouge foncé avec écusson de béret de Régiment de parachutistes. Il porte un AK-47 ce qui suggère qu'il appartient à un bataillon de commando de parachutistes.

D1 Uniforme de camouflage unique en son genre avec ailes de parachutiste et écusson de qualification de commando mais sans autre insigne. **D2** Camouflage DPM indien avec poches et chaussures de grande tenue. Ailes de parachutiste sur la poche droite et écusson de qualification de commando sur la poche droite. **D3** Camouflage DPM indien avec poches en toile verte de fabrication indienne pour porter des chargeurs supplémentaires pour sa version du fusil FN FAL de 7,62 mm de fabrication indienne.

E1 Ensemble vert de grande tenue de l'Armée indienne; le turban bleu foncé/rouge et l'écusson de casquette doré sont des pièces standard pour les officiers Sikhs de grade général. Il porte un insigne de rang de général de division sur les épaules et le 'poignard ailé' de la SFF sur l'épaule gauche. **E2** Commando tibétain comme du treillis standard de l'Armée indienne et un casque noir avec nom inscrit au pochoir sur celui-ci. Il porte un Mk 4 Sterling et les initiales 'SFF' sur les deux épaules tandis que l'insigne de la formation SFF est sur l'épaule gauche et l'aile de parachutiste SFF sur la droite. **E3** Sur le signe de la formation qui est distribué depuis la formation de la SFF en 1962 apparaît le lion des neiges mythique du Tibet et l'épée tibétaine flamboyante.

F1 Veste à fermeture éclair noire et gilet pare-balles britannique. Il porte une radio dans la poche de la manche droite et un MP-5 A2 Heckler & Koch avec lame additionnelle fixée en style duplex. **F2** Treillis et casque noirs et gilet pare-balles britannique. Il porte un fusil de tireur d'élite PSG-1 de 7,62 mm Heckler & Koch avec visées télescopiques. **F3** Ecusson de "Chat Noir" du Groupe de Gardes Montés Spécial NSG porté sur l'épaule gauche.

G1 Ce commando est armé d'une arbalète commerciale avec visée de fabrication américaine. Insigne de formation IMSF porté sur l'épaule droite contrairement à la pratique indienne courante. **G2** Camouflage DPM indien avec turban gris olivâtre, porté par les Sikhs pendant les opérations. Il porte un Mk4 Sterling de fabrication indienne avec chargeurs supplémentaires dans une poche indienne sur la poitrine.

H1 Blouse de camouflage DPM britannique, badge de béret SSG sur écusson bleu clair, titres métalliques SSG sur les épaules, aile SSG portée sur la poche droite. Pour arme, un fusil d'assaut 56-1 de type chinois. **H2** Chemise DPM britannique, armure de corps occidentale et masque à gaz. Il porte une mitraillette MP-5 A3 H & K. Les titres métalliques sur les épaules sont les seuls insignes SSG portés.

Farbtafeln

A1 Schwarzer Absprunganzug, Helm, Armband-Höhenmesser, rechteckiger Fallschirm mit amerikanischem Laub-Tarnmuster. Bewaffnet mit 7,62 mm SLR 'Commando' Pistole; die Western Command-Insignien auf der Schulter kennzeichnen ihn als Angehörigen des 10. Para Commando-Bataillons. **A2** Eine exakte Kopie des britischen SAS-Abzeichens miit dem Motto "Opfer" in Hindi. **A3** Schwarze Uniform mit schwarzem Stirnband und einer indischen 7,62 mm Nachtzielfernrohr aus den USA.

B1 Standard-Winterkapuzenjacke mit Schneebrillen. Bewaffnet mit einer sowjetischen Flugzeugabwehrrakete SA-7; Insignien der Gebirgsdivision auf der linken Schulter.

C1 Normale grüne indische Armeeuniform mit Divisionsabzeichen auf der linken Schulter und einem Kunststoff-Namensschild über der rechten Tasche. Kappenabzeichen des 11. Gurkha-Regiments. **C2** Kaki-Uniform der indischen Armee mit rotbrauner Baskenmütze, die Abzeichen des Fallschirmjägerregiments trägt. Bewaffnet mit einer AK-47, was andeutet, dass er einem Fallschirmjägerkommandoregiment angehört.

D1 Eine einmalige Tarnuniform mit Fallschirmjägerschwingen und Qualifikationsabzeichen für Kommandos; keine sonstigen Insignien. **D2** Indische DPM-Tarnuniform und Ausgehschuhe. Fallschirmjägerschwingen über der rechten Tasche, auf der sich das Kommando-Qualifikationsabzeichen befindet. **D3** Indische DPM-Tarnuniform mit Segeltuchtaschen indischer Machart für Reservemagazine für seine indische Version des 7,62 mm-Gewehrs FN FAL.

E1 Grüne indische Ausgehuniform; dunkelblau/roter Turban mit Goldabzeichen für Sikh-Offiziere im Generalsrang. Er trägt die Rangabzeichen eines Generalmajors auf den Schultern; auf der linken Schulter der SFF-'Schwingen-Dolch'. **E2** Tibetischer Kommando-Angehöriger mit der indischen Standard-Feldunform und einem schwarzen Helm mit Namensaufschrift. Bewaffnet mit einer Sterling Mk 4, trägt er die Buchstaben 'SFF' auf beiden Schultern, Das SFF-Formationsabzeichen auf der linken und die SFF-Fallschirmjägerschwinge auf der rechten Schulter. **E3** Das Formationsabzeichen – erschienen seit Gründung der SFF 1962 – zeigt den legendären tibetischen Schneelöwen und ein flammendes tibetisches Schwert.

F1 Schwarze Jacke mit Reissverschluss und britische kugelsichere Weste. Er trägt ein Funkgerät in der rechten Armtasche und eine Heckler & Koch MP-5 A2-Maschinenpistole mit angehängtem Reservemagazin. **F2** Schwarze Dienstuniform und Helm sowie eine britische kugelsichere Weste. Er trägt ein Scharfschützen gewehr Heckler & Koch 7,62 mm PSG-1 mit Zielfernrohr. **F3** 'Black Cat'-Abzeichen der NSG Special Ranger Group auf der linken Schulter.

G1 Dieser Kommando-Kämpfer ist mit einer kommerziell in den USA hergestellten Armbrust mit Zielfernrohr ausgerüstet. Das IMSF-Formationsabzeichen wird im Gegensatz zur normalgen indischen Art auf der rechten Schulter getragen. **G2** Indische DPM-Tarnuniform mit olivfarbenem Turban, wie ihn Sikhs im Einsatz tragen. Er trägt eine in Indien hergestellte Sterling Mk4, mit Reservemagazin in einer indischen Tasche auf der Brust.

H1 Britische DPM-Tarnjacke, SSG-Baskenmützenabzeichen auf einem hellblauen Blitz, SSG-Abzeichen aus Metall auf den Schultern und SSG-Schwinge über der rechten Tasche. Bewaffnet mit Sturmgewehr 56-1 nach chinesischer Art. **H2** Britisches DPM-Hemd, Westliche Kugelschutzweste und Gasmaske. Err trägt eine Maschinenpistole H&K MP-5 A3. Als einzige SSG-Insignien die in Metall auf der Schulter.

I1 Camouflage US avec écusson 'PAK ARMY' au-dessus de la poche gauche, insigne de formation SSG sur l'épaule gauche, ailes SSG de monteur-régleur au-dessus de la poche droite. I2 Treillis marrons courants de l'Armée pakistanaise, poche de poitrine de fabrication chinoise pour chargeurs AK-47 et écusson de qualification de guerre en montagne sur l'épaule droite. Pour arme un fusil d'assaut de type chinois 56-1. I3 Insigne de qualification de chute libre et de guerre en montagne sur l'épaule droite et ailes SSG sur la poche droite.

J1 Treillis beiges SSGN courants, ancre engagée de la Marine pakistanaise sur l'épaule gauche, insigne de qualification de plongée sur la poche droite. Ecusson de coiffure rouge de la Marine pakistanaise porté un béret bleu/pourpre SSGN indiquant qu'il s'agit d'un sous-officier. Pour arme le fusil G3 Heckler & Koch. J2 Sous officier SSGN avec fusil G3 de 7,62 mm Heckler & Koch, sac de campagne de distribution standard de l'armée pakistanaise et gilet de sauvetage autour du cou.

K1 Treillis standard vert olive avec bottes fabriquées à Sri Lanka. Ecusson de qualification de commando sur la poche droite; au-dessus ailes de saut. Ecusson de Régiment de Commando sur le béret rouge foncé et écussons jaunes sur les deux épaules avec le mot 'Commando' écrit en cingalais. Pour arme le 56-1 de type chinois. K2 Uniforme de travail marron foncé STF avec ceinturon vert et boucle ronde en argent. Sur les deux épaules écusson de la police de Sri Lanka et un autre avec 'Corps expéditionnaire spécial' sur la poche droite. L'officier présenté ici porte le béret vert STF avec écusson en tissu de la police. Les insignes de rang de la police se portent sur les épaules. K3 Uniforme de camouflage DPM britannique et casquette assortie. Il porte un lance-grenades Armscor sud-africain de 40 mm, à six coups, et un M-16.

L1 Les commandos afghans portent les ailes des unités aéroportées à droite sur la poitrine; on a vu plusieurs versions y compris un simple insigne métallique, cousu et des ailes en métal sur un fond de toile en couleur. Les commandos portent un béret rouge foncé avec un grand écusson métallique de l'armée afghane. L'insigne de formation du commando se porte sur l'épaule droite. L2 Il est porté par toutes les formations de commando, y est inscrit en pouchtou le mot 'commando' transcrit phonétiquement. L3 Jusqu'au début des années 1980 l'écusson du calot de bataillon de parachutistes présentait Bhairab Nath, le dieu du ciel hindou, que l'on voit ici; les mots 'Bhairab Nath' sont imprimés au bas. L4 Ecusson actuel pour les bataillons de parachutistes sur ses chapeaux Gurkha.

I1 US-Tarnuniform mit Abzeichen 'PAK ARMY' über linker Tasche, SSG-Formationsabzeichen auf linker Schulter, SSG-Riggerschwingen über echter Tasche. I2 Braune pakistanische Standard-ArmeeuniformChinesische Brusttasche für AK-47-Magazin und Gebirgskrieg-Qualifikationsabzeichen auf rechter Schulter. Bewaffnet mit Sturmgewehr 56-1 chinesischer Art. I3 Fallschirmjäger- und Gebirgskrieg-Qualifikationsabzeichen auf rechter Schulter, SSG-Schwingen über rechter Tasche.

J1 Beige SSGN-Standard-Dienstuniform, unklarer Anker der pakistanischen Kriegsmarine auf linker Schulter, Taucher-Qualifikationsabzeichen auf der rechten. Rotes Kappenabzeichen der pakistanischen Marine auf blauer/violetter SSGN-Baskenmütze zeigt Unteroffiziersrang an. Bewaffnet mit H&K 7,62 mm G3-Gewehr; Standard-Armeeranzen und Schwimmweste um den Hals.

K1 Olivgrüne Standard-Dienstuniform mit Stiefeln aus Sri Lanka. Kommando-Qualifikationsabzeichen über rechter Tasche; darüber Absprungschwingen. Kappenabzeichen des Commando-Regiments auf rotbrauner Mütze, gelbe Spangen auf beiden Schultern mit Aufschrift 'Kommando' in singhalesischer Schrift. Bewaffnet mit der chinesischen 56-1. K2 Dunkelbraune STF-Dienstuniform mit grünem Gürtel und runder silberner Schnalle. Auf beiden Schultern trägt er ein Abzeichen der Polizei von Sri Lanka, und über die rechte Tasche verläuft eine Spange mit der Aufschrift 'Special Task Force' (Spezialeinsatztruppe). Der Offizier trägt die grüne SRF-Baskenmütze mit Polizeiabzeichen aus Stoff. K3 Britische DPM-Tarnuniform mit passender Kappe. Er ist bewaffnet mit einem südafrikanischen 40 mm-Granatwerfer Armscor und einer M-16.

L1 Afghanische Kommandos tragen Luftlandeschwingen über der rechten Brusttasche in verschiedenen Versionen: einfaches Metall, genähter Bullion oder Metallschwingen mit farbiger Stoffunterlage. Sie tragen ferner rotbraune Mützen mit grossem Armeeabzeichen aus Metall. Kommando-Formationsinsignien auf der rechten Schulter. L2 Von allen Kommando-Formationen getragen: das englische Wort 'Commando', phonetisch auf Pushtun übersetzt. L3 Bis Anfang der 80er Jahre trug Fallschirmjäger-Kappenabzeichen den Hindu-Windgott Bhairab Nath, wie hier; der Name steht darunter. L4 Jetziges Abzeichen für die Gurkha-Hüte des Fallschirmjäger-Bataillons.